Surviving Your First Years in the Classroom

Survive your first years as a teacher with the no-nonsense tips and stories in this book. Learn how to choose respect over being liked, content over cute, grace over grades, and planning over Pinterest. Also find out how to avoid the teacher's lounge mentality and surround yourself with positive influences. The author's honest tone and humor throughout will leave you feeling inspired and ready to tackle the challenges that can come your way, so you can stay happy in your role and remember why you chose a career in education.

Bonus: The book features a variety of worksheets you can use immediately, on lesson planning, student behavior and motivation, and more.

Jordan McKinney is a second grade teacher in Pensacola, Florida. She has worked as a math intervention specialist, fourth grade teacher, and first grade teacher. She was named Teacher of the Year in 2019. Follow her on Instagram at @sunshinestateteacher.

Also Available from Routledge Eye On Education

Your First Year: How to Survive and Thrive as a New Teacher
Todd Whitaker, Madeline Whitaker, Katherine Whitaker

Classroom Management from the Ground Up
Todd Whitaker, Madeline Whitaker, Katherine Whitaker

The First-Year English Teacher's Guidebook: Strategies for Success
Sean Ruday

The Edupreneur's Side Hustle Handbook: 10 Successful Educators Share Their Top Tips
Lisa Dunnigan and Tosha Wright

Get Money for Your Classroom: Easy Grant Writing Ideas That Work
Barbara Gottschalk

Classroom Instruction from A to Z
Barbara R. Blackburn

Passionate Learners: How to Engage and Empower Your Students
Pernille Ripp

Surviving Your First Years in the Classroom

Twelve Brutally Honest Tips for Elementary Teachers

Jordan McKinney

Routledge
Taylor & Francis Group

NEW YORK AND LONDON

First published 2021
by Routledge
52 Vanderbilt Avenue, New York, NY 10017

and by Routledge
2 Park Square, Milton Park, Abingdon, Oxon, OX14 4RN

Routledge is an imprint of the Taylor & Francis Group, an informa business

© 2021 Jordan McKinney

Library of Congress Cataloging-in-Publication Data
A catalog record for this title has been requested

ISBN: 978-0-367-63597-8 (hbk)
ISBN: 978-0-367-63465-0 (pbk)
ISBN: 978-1-003-11987-6 (ebk)

Typeset in Palatino
by codeMantra

Contents

Opening Letter

Dear Educator,

I'm just like you. My heart is filled with the names of all the students who have walked through my door, and those who have yet to. I live on the bright colors of flair pens and scented markers. I dream of being the person a little kid hops onto the school bus eager to see.

I AM A TEACHER.

I have had my heart bruised from rough days with parents and students, and have been so busy my coffee sits on my desk cold. I struggle to learn the new rules that the governing powers set for us, and try to learn quickly to adapt. I have sat wondering where did I go wrong and did I pick the right profession. Then quickly those moments fade with a hug from a former student and reading a warm and fuzzy note from a prior year.

We, teachers, are in for the fight of our lives when it comes to the field of education. We are like soldiers on the front line of a war, and we have to be prepared to fight. If you are currently a teacher, then I am glad to have you on my team, and if you are new to the battlefield, then I welcome you. You are in for the most beautiful experience of your life. During my beginning years in the journey of education, I made so many small and silly mistakes. I earned my battle scars and earned them well.

So I guess that is why I am writing this book to you. So that maybe you my dear friend don't have to make those mistakes. That you can take what I have stumbled upon over these years and then run with it. I don't know everything, but what I do know I want to share with you. I hope that it can help make a difference for you as you enter your classroom.

You and I, we are teammates and know that I am sending prayers and positive thoughts your way as you read this. Stick with this path that you are on. This profession is the greatest gift in the world, and you are lucky enough to have found it. Keep loving kids well, perfecting your craft, and shining bright for all to see and you can't go wrong.

Best Wishes,
Mrs. McKinney

Introduction

What is it about failing that leads to success?

In a drawer in my desk sits a few very important notes that I keep locked away for the days I need to remember my first years as a teacher. You're probably nodding saying, "yes, we all have those similar positive notes for the hard days." However, mine are not those. They are the notes that represent my failures in those first years as a teacher. I have notes that state, "I'm sorry we made you cry Miss Baggett," or "We will be better tomorrow." At the time I read these years ago they tugged on my heart, and now they absolutely break it.

It would be easy to throw them away, but to me that would be almost like a lie. Like applying a coat of wax to my early years as a teacher and buffing them out. I read these, because they are a reminder of where I began. Of the struggles and lessons I have gained within the confines of my classrooms. They remind me of days with tears in my eyes, and me wanting to pull my hair out thinking, "I can't do this!" When we have these tokens that remind us of the strength we've gained, it can propel us into the future with new found courage. It's like an old mirror held up to my former reflection.

I was the absolute worst. It's nearly as bad as looking at the makeup you used to think looked great in middle school. At the moment? Wonderful! In hindsight, it is incredibly painful to look at. Abdul Kalam says the quote we teachers know and preach by. That failure simply means, "First. Attempt. In. Learning."[1] I think back on all the little moments that I nearly left the teaching profession and somehow God opened a window. I went from being the literal bottom of the hill, crying to my job every morning, to where I am now. I am the current

Teacher of the Year at my school. I work within two blocks of the beach and teach my dream grade which is second. I wake up with a pep in my step and ready to go off and see my students, and anticipate meeting my students at the end of summer. Suffice to say that my days look very different. So this book is for you. Those of us in the profession wondering the question, "Will this get better?" My question back for you is, do you want it to?

If you're saying yes! I want to make it through these first years of teaching with my sanity intact and my heart still in it, then hopefully this book helps. I will share with you my failures and how, despite being the worst version of myself, I found my way to my dream. When I look back at these notes, I want to go back to my younger self. To give her a hug, wipe the tears, and to tell her, "it's not like this forever. Even more so YOU my dear will get better. The world may not change but your practice and heart need to before you can continue. It's all going to be great."

I want to be the friend to her that I just didn't have at that time. To be like the friend we all know who you take shopping, because you know they will tell you if that top is actually cute. It stings when they share the truth, but you can breathe easier because you know you're on the right path. I didn't have that person in education then to be my confidant or truth speaker, and so maybe I can be yours.

I am going to give you the 12 things I learned as an educator that I wish someone would've told me bluntly as I fumbled through my years of teaching. Some of my stories are embarrassing, and some are painful. However, each gives you a bit of insight into how/why I believe this tip is useful and how you can implement this into your own classroom. Now all I ask of you is this. As you read these stories read them with an open heart and mind. Step back and ask yourself, "Do I fall for these same missteps?" Then see if any of these tips and techniques can help make your day even just a bit better.

I believe self-critiquing is where we find our best selves. You can only improve and enjoy your career as much as you are willing to try. There is a light at the end of the tunnel when it comes to those years that are incredibly rough. I hope this book will guide you as you find your way through the darkness.

Note

1 "A Quote by A.P.J. Abdul Kalam." *Goodreads*, Goodreads, www.goodreads. com/quotes/1015959---if-you-fail-never-give-up-because-f-a-i-l-means.

1

Planning over Pinterest

How can I set myself up for successful before the year even begins?

I'll be honest with you all. This part is hard for me to admit and write. You may read this section and either sympathize or may hate me. Honestly, I can't control what you feel for the younger version of myself. Honestly? I really pity and dislike her. She got out of college with her head in the clouds and visions of the movie *Waiting for Superman* in her eyes.

I think a lot of teachers have been at this moment. I think of it more as the savior complex. You're going to swoop into the classroom. It'll look perfect and you will know just what to do. You'll read a few books, teach a few lessons, and get up on your desk like in the *Dead Poets Society* and these kids' lives will change just like you've always dreamed of, right? Now those of us who've even taught a couple of years have either made that mistake and are nodding in unison of "yes, and what dummies we were," or may have set this book down in thought of, "man what a weirdo." To which I agree with both statements.

I went into teaching with the best of intentions. I knew since I was five years old, I wanted to become a teacher. Hanging in my classroom currently is a little art project from first grade that reads, "My dream is to become a teacher to change a life. I know it'll be tough, but I want to become a teacher." Somewhere along the way, I must've forgotten the, "it'll be the tough part," though

I couldn't have imagined how tough my first class would be and how poorly I would handle it. Now to keep this all locked up and safe I will be changing the names of all schools, students, and coworkers. You need to know the stories to get why I'm telling you it gets better and how.

I started my first job in a low-income school on the rougher side of my hometown. I was to be the new first grade teacher. My first classroom was a bumblebee theme to coincide with my then B last name. I was so excited. As I walked in for my tour of the school (I had interviewed on the phone) the janitor and fellow teacher mentioned, "this is a revolving door school." Though I know it now, was naive then, it was probably being said to me as in, "aw honey, you won't last the year." In my mind, I was thinking that it was so upsetting and that I wanted to make a change.

I spent the short week or two that I had to prepare all in designing my room and collecting books to add to a library. I set up bulletin boards, taped up posters, and added shelf paper to old bookcases. My favorite piece being a board in the hall that boasted a "Look at This Bee-utiful Work!" and had clothes pins with cute bee's hanging on the butter yellow fabric. In full disclosure within the first nine weeks a student in an angry rage literally football punted those bee's down the hall with my principal watching. I think that might've nearly broken me as I saw those cute bee faces smashing on the floor. However, before school began, I felt naively that all these décor pieces and books were going to help me succeed. I bet you can guess how that panned out. It did not go as expected.

The supply drops off went swimmingly and I was pumped to begin. Even my mentors with the county were feeling great about my room and the preparedness of my materials and that ever more boosted my self-confidence. When it comes to organization my type-A self really has always had that down. It was all looking so promising. That's the beauty of the days before the school year starts, visions of kumbaya moments with your students dance in your heads. However, that came crashing down the instant that Monday began.

I had a class of 18 first graders. Their adorable faces entered my room, and my horrible classroom management began. I can't even honestly remember what my rules were. They were all about making classroom contracts at our school through the program Capturing Kids Hearts and so I hadn't really thought about actual rules. While I bumbled through countless mistakes, we all make, I met a few kids that I'll never forget. The one that lives in infamy was Jason. My roommate at the time still brings him up when we reminisce on our first years in our jobs. He was cute with the sweetest face you've ever seen. That was until a dark look overcame his face. Then the real terror of the day began. It would go from throwing desks, screaming, clawing at the door as he was taken to the counselor, etc. You name it and it probably happened. I remember a meltdown after he got a B on a spelling test and I took my kids to do yoga in the field as he ripped apart the room and was taken down the hall. You know in a scary movie where someone is gripping the banister instead of being dragged somewhere? The screaming and clawing that's going on? Yeah, that's how this was. It took four large men to get him out of my room during those tantrums.

Where it got really rough was during a day at carpet time. In the middle of reading my story of the day he got up and kicked another student right in the mouth I could feel the room just freeze. To my horror, I bolted up to press the intercom. At that moment I realized to my dread that it wasn't working. Of course, right? So, I picked up the classroom phone to dial the office for assistance. At that moment (probably due to fear of getting in trouble) Jason came up behind me and yanked my head back by grabbing fistfuls of hair tugging my head away from the phone. The woman in the office said she could only hear my screams on the other line. As strands of my hair found their way ripped from my head, he also found his way out of my room. The rest of the class still remained on the carpet frozen in fear of what they'd witnessed. When my mentor came the next day she was told, "I thought she would be gone after yesterday," from the principal. I was promised the intercom would be fixed and this wouldn't happen again. I can safely say it wasn't repaired in the time I remained there.

Now Jason wasn't the only kiddo in my class that had some scary moments. The other friend of mine that I will always remember was Andy. He was also one that had his two Dr. Jekyll and Mr. Hyde sides. You were able to tell as he walked down the hall which side was out for the day. One day he walked up to my mentor during observation and said, "I'm scared." To which of course she asked, "of what dear?" He looked at her and said shyly, "Of what the voices in my head tell me to do." Yep. Really creepy stuff going on there. He'd crawl on desks like a tiger and growl, and this was with the vice principal watching. Eventually, he was baker acted and taken to the hospital with a police escort to make sure the mother got him there safely. He was back in my room after he was released several days later. At the time I was 22 and absolutely terrified of all these weird experiences in my class, and now I feel sadness for all those kids must have been enduring.

Now those are only two of the few stories from that class. There were honestly many others that I experience as do many educators every day. That is a battle all of us may face at some time or another. However, this is where I look back and regret so much that I did. Yes, I had some crazy students. However, looking back I wish someone had said to me, "Your classroom is the chaos you create." The reality is I was the reason those kids may have gotten to that level of crazy. Why? Simply because I should've followed my first tip.

Tip #1
Planning
Over
Pinterest

I fell for this mistake during my first few years in the classroom. I would dream and look up the cutest classroom styles, behavior plans, first day activities, classroom songs, and really anything I would call fluff. What did I forget to look up? That would be what I was going to do after the first day. We get lost in the Pinterest perfect sides of things that we forget to get out of the book and really focus on the nit and grit of daily life in the classroom.

If that year I had come in with the mentality of how I was going to hold those students accountable, I believe I may not have lost those strands of hair. Instead, I was so focused on my bumble bee themed room and the packets parents received at the supply drop off that I barely had cracked a textbook. My friend, as much as that Pinterest board of cuteness may call to you and you tell yourself, "but it will create a warm and inviting space," trust me when I say you and your kids will not care one week into the year.

Bright and shiny classrooms are not what makes for a successful school year. I remember feeling overwhelmed by the need to have as cute of a room as my fellow educators. I wish I had just been told, "the kids won't care." The weeks you are preparing for class sit down and turn off the computer. Open your teacher editions, write out your procedures, finalize those simple few rules, and relax. Your kids will love more your clean routines in a blank room, than hung up decorations in the middle of chaos.

There are still times where even now that I know this, I will catch myself getting lost in the void of bright colored rooms and perfectly laid out materials. I mean what teacher can resist a perfectly curated classroom? Then I remind myself that my time is best spent on the construction of my management and curriculum than the creation of bulletin boards for birthdays.

So, you may be walking into that brand-new room. The four walls are bare or left with the miscellaneous items the teacher before you left. There's that excitement that is building but also the pounding in your heart of what to do next. First off before you run to the teacher store to buy that fadeless paper, let's sit down and go over the finer details that you'll need to make that year a smashing success!

The How To
Let's
Start
Planning!

1.1 Find Your Vibe

Now I'm sure you've probably thought of a classroom theme. Here's the thing. I'm not saying a theme is 100% necessary. However, having a staple color, signature item, or design makes the flow of your classroom so much easier. For example, my theme is pineapples with the colors teal, yellow, and pink. So, when I go to the store or I create worksheets for parents, everything follows those few items. Why does that matter? Nothing looks better than when a quick clip art ties something together. Heck, you could just love the color purple and always print your newsletters on purple paper! This just helps you save some money by not buying a ton of useless items that don't go together. It keeps you on a central track with your selections, and kids love it. Just make sure you pick a color or item you actually like. Your collection will grow, and now I have more pineapple cups, mugs, and knick knacks than I could've imagined!

1.2 You Rule

Don't you move another step into your design process without deciding your three to five classroom rules! Your room can be completely bare except for your rules and do much better than the Pinterest classroom down the hall that doesn't have a firm set of them. That's all you need is three to five key ideas that kids will memorize. Don't go over that or honestly the little ones will never remember them.

My favorite way to come up with my rules is to use an acronym. Remember that vibe I mentioned earlier? Have your rules fit that similar feel. My classroom is two blocks from the crystal blue waters of the Gulf of Mexico. So, my rules are the acronym BEACH! It's cute and simple, and with a poster board and some pineapples I am good to go! My school has even adopted my rules since I joined the faculty in 2017.

Be kind to others

Eyes and ears are listening

Alert and ready to learn

Classmates are family

Hands and feet to yourself

Here's another fun tip! I have my students memorize the rule for a treat on the Friday of the first week of school. We practice all week and create hand motions for each rule together. This way the students take ownership of the rules, even though I created them. So yes, my students have the rules memorized, but that's not even the best part!

Let's say in the middle of a lesson Jenny is talking too much. I don't want to embarrass her in front of her peers, but really Jenny needs to stop talking! I simply look at her and discreetly make the signal they came up with for "Eyes and Ears are Listening." Then boom! She is quiet and back on task. I don't have any tears, embarrassment, and she knows Mrs. McKinney means business! On the recess field I can call out "Rule #5," and they know hands up and off one another. I spend less time correcting and more time teaching.

1.3 Map Out Your Procedures

Here's something about kids that we sometimes forget. Kids have to be told exactly what to do and have that broken down in the steps. There is no simply walk down the hall. It is broken into walk directly behind the person in front of you, with your hands to your side, mouths closed, and to the side of the hallway. Yet this was something I didn't realize until I would tell my first graders just to simply sharpen their pencils when they needed to. Big mistake! You haven't seen crazy until you see kids in a mob fighting for the sharpener. It's as scary as people fighting for the tv on sale at Walmart on Black Friday after Thanksgiving.

Not only do you need rules in your classroom, you need procedures for everything from bathroom breaks to how to get a tissue. In the bustle of the school year beginning these simple tasks can get lost in the fray of welcome packets. So, to make it simple, I have shared my check list of tasks that you should sit and plan out before pre planning even begins. Some of these maybe things that you think aren't truly necessary to review, but even the older kids and beyond need to know how to ask for help lest you have kids yelling your name in the middle of an exam or lesson.

Take these procedures in this book and during that first week of school pick two to three a day to practice. Do an activity, then a procedure, and then back to do something fun to break it up. There is never such a thing as too much practice, and as my principal would say, "perfect practice is what makes perfect."

1.4 Parent Communication

Your students' parents can be either your greatest ally or your toughest hurdle. What determines which they will be is up to your communication with them. Your students' parents never go into a year wanting the teacher to be terrible. You have to keep that in mind as you begin planning for the year. Some may just not click with you, more on that later, but don't let a lack of communication be a problem when it comes to your relationship. Have a tool in place and practice it before your year begins. While email is great, there are plenty of applications out there that make sharing the classroom experience with their child a breeze.

	Unlimited Message Length	Messaging to Group	Message to Individual Parents	Classroom Management	Portfolio of Student Work
Seesaw	✓	✓	✓		✓
Bloomz	✓	✓	✓	✓	✓
Class Dojo				✓	
Remind		✓	✓		

Personally, I use the website Seesaw for my students' parents. I try to send out a Monday Memo to everyone weekly and add at least a few activities done by their child a week through the photo feature. A parent shouldn't hear from you the first time and it is because their child got into trouble.

1.5 Behavior Plan

So, you have your rules and procedures, but beyond those how will you keep your students accountable? Let me say this. No behavior plan is perfect, but the one you will stick to is the best. I remember my second year, I had this beautiful bulletin board that aligned with the behavior app Class Dojo. When the kids did well, they earned a point, and if not, they lost one. I had this grand idea of having a store with coupons for the kids to earn with their points and shop each week. I was so excited.

Then the first week to shop loomed around and the kids spent some of their dojo dollars. Then week two came up, and we were so busy we missed it that week. Another week came and yet again I completely forgot. By this point the dojo dollar was worthless, because they never believed they would be rewarded. Students are only as excited as you are when it comes to rewards. Suffice to say that reward system wasn't great for me.

I ended up finally finding that Whole Brain Teaching worked best with my teaching style and created my own reward system based on the Pensacola area. I created levels that fit each icon in Pensacola. As they earn points for going above expectations, they earn points. At each level they earn a reward based on the theme of that icon. For example, in Pensacola we have a bridge called the Graffiti Bridge. It's a local icon and thus the level is called Graffiti Artist, and they get a can of silly string. I have added the point sheet in the back of this book as well as what is on the back of the sheet which are self-reflection pieces that they fill out on those rough days. The level they are on the wall is displayed on a door using sand dollars that are printed on bright color paper to match the improvers' wall. I was surprised to find that I could keep up with the beach themed program, and so my kids bought in and stuck to it.

Don't just settle for a clip chart. Those embarrass your students and are becoming a way of the past. How would you feel if your name was on the "do better wall" at work for all to see? You probably wouldn't feel so good. So, while it's tempting to settle into what our teachers used to do, I implore you to research what behavior plan works with your personality. Most importantly, is this something you can keep up with or will you need to do a good bit of prep work? Be honest with yourself and stick to what you choose.

1.6 Classroom Layout

I wish there was a magical way to set up our classrooms to know ahead of time that we were going to have a successful year. That we knew that Sam and Sarah would chit chat and can't sit next to each other, or that Drake needs to be in the back, so he doesn't distract others. These are the things you learn and figure out as you and your students become a family. While you cannot prepare for who your new students will be, you can plan for how the room will be arranged to set you up for the best possible outcome.

Take the time to sketch out the layout of your room. Where will you have circle time or come together for presentations? Where will you store certain materials? Do you plan to have groups or have your students in rows? Similar to how I mentioned earlier that you should have procedures in place for everything, you should also have in mind the movement and focus of your classroom.

When it comes to bulletin boards, pick something functional. For example, I have a board that I use to show off student work. Or have a board that is for items you don't change often such as classroom rules or procedures. Mistakes I have made include planning for a bulletin board that I have to change often or expect to interact with more. Sometimes I just don't have the time to change out a board. If it's between that and planning an experiment, the experiment wins in a landslide!

Little decisions from where you plan for the sharpener to be the placement of the manipulatives for easy access can make your day run a lot more smoothly. Don't waste space with random posters and knick knacks from the dollar spot (though I love them) they get in the way! Once you have a better understanding of the practical side of your room, you can pour your teacher's version of Joanna Gaines heart out and get to prepping!

1.7 Homework

I don't think I've ever heard more of a hot button topic amongst teachers than homework and how much to give it. I have seen the debates on Facebook forums, and even amongst staff in schools I've taught in. People will fight over who gives too much and who gives too little. There isn't a perfect answer when it comes to your rule on homework.

You may be thinking, well okay so why even bring it up? If you don't have the perfect solution then what help are you? The reality is there isn't a perfect solution, but there is your teaching philosophy and what aligns with it. You have to sit back, read the research, see all of the options, and decide what is best for your ideals and your kiddos. When your students' parents come to ask you why you assign what you do, all you can do is have the data and research to back up why you do what you do.

Personally, I assign all of my students work on Monday and they have the week to complete it. So no complaints that they had soccer and were out late one night. They have the week to plan around those things. I align what I assign to my kids from standards we are learning in class. I've yet to have any issues, and I have a no tears policy. If they feel like there's going to be some frustrated tears I tell my kids to stop, and see me the next day.

Find your own homework vision and reason and stick to it. Those first weeks of school will fly by and you'll need to assign work before you know it. Just make sure what you assign isn't busy work and will enrich your students' education or support it.

1.8 How You Begin and How You End

We know that first impressions are everything, and that it's not how you begin but how you finish. These ideals we hear in various portions of our life, but they can also dive over into the classroom. I can vividly remember mornings filled with tiny children rushing into the room and diving straight into the curriculum and working up until that final bell. It didn't give us the feeling of excitement as one might get before the big game or leave us feeling fulfilled with the day. Those last moments before your students board the bus are the ones that they will remember when their parents asked them how their day was. So, when planning for those morning and end of day meetings I think of the four P's.

Positive
Planned
Practical
Process

◆ Planned- Make sure that you set aside in your schedule the time that you want to allot for this beginning
and end of the day meeting. It doesn't need to be more
than ten minutes, but it can have a lasting impact. Plan
out what you want to use the time for. I do "brownies"
so what their best part of the day was. I've also had us
learn a Spanish word of the day, give each other compliments, play games with math facts, or read from our
class novel. Whatever you choose to use just make sure
that you have something in mind. If you get to the carpet
at the end of the day without a plan, they are going to go
bananas!

◆ Practical- Make sure that what you use this time for is
something you can do without a ton of prep or time. This
probably isn't the time to have to pull any materials out,
because once you begin teaching or the bell rings you
gotta get moving! Always ask what your "why" is for
a task in your room. For example, playing games with
math facts is always a hit because they not only need the
review, but they have a ton of fun!

◆ Process- Imagine your student gets home and they are
asked what they did at school. I bet you can guess in one
try what they are going to say. Right! "Nothing." It's like
a knife to our educator hearts! We think of all the things
we did in the day: the experiments, math games, class
novels, songs we learned, etc. and wonder how they
could say that simple word! Honestly sometimes kids
just forget, and even high schoolers do too. They are consumed with getting to their after school fun activities and
so talking about what they did isn't really a priority. To
increase your chances of getting a few less "nothings,"
have your students process with you what they learned
right before the bell. You can ask questions such as: What
did you learn? Why is that important? How would you
explain that to others? This may also help firmly implant
those wonderful lessons you spent hours cultivating.

◆ Positive- Make sure that no matter how the day went
you end on a positive note. A simple "I love you" can

be all that needs to be said. Kids sometimes go home to the worst of circumstances without you knowing. Even if they were a little bit off their rocker you don't know who needs that little bit of compassion before they walk out. It can be sharing a compliment a day to one student, or having them give shout outs, or just having a class saying. Remember that they need to be loved no matter how much you want to pull your hair out.

How you begin and end your classroom day is going to be the defining piece of how your students view your class. A simple sit down and planning of these moments and the materials you may need can set you up for success prior to your first day!

1.9 Curriculum and Apps

Take time before you hit the shops and Pinterest to see what materials you have and which you need. If you aren't really going to be teaching a ton on one particular skill don't get sucked into the dollar spot and find yourself buying a ton of manipulatives you don't need. Here's an example. When I worked in Charlotte during the summer before I began teaching, my friends and I would hit up the local yard sales. I would get so excited finding books for amazing deals. I found a Percy Jackson series for five dollars and a book on American history for two. I was pumped at what a great teacher shopper I was.

Then I got my first teaching assignment which was first grade. So what help were those books? They weren't going to do me a lick of good. I purchased materials I never used, and once my bank account was barely holding enough for my rent, I realized I had spent money in places for my room that I didn't need, with nothing left over to help buy items I did.

Look up the standards for the grades you teach. I know they aren't as exciting as Pinterest, but knowing what you are actually required to teach is essential. Then you can write out what skills you don't have the manipulatives or supplies for, and go out with a better idea of where to spend your time and money.

1.10 Own It and Sell It

What does a used car salesman and a teacher have in common?

They can both sell you on any idea.

Teaching and sales aren't so different. You have to sell what you're doing to your students' parents and the students themselves. The best part of if? If you make something a big deal, it becomes a BIG DEAL!

In my class I have made the rank of Blue Angel on our super improvers board the greatest achievement of all time. I buy four dollars pins and show those babies off like they are the heart of the ocean from Titanic. My students literally dream all year of earning one of those pins. They aren't worth more than a Starbucks latte, but man are they effective? The same goes for pencil cap erasers. My students can buy them for one classroom dollar. You'd think those things were worth more. I pump them up, and so my kids are paying their bucks left and right to form a collection.

You are your own biggest cheerleader. The more you sell an idea, the more your students will buy into it. Anything from this list I've written can only be made stronger if you sell it. If you make being the quietest class in the hallway the coolest thing, man those kids will tip toe! You gush over sharing compliments at the end of the day? They will fight over themselves to raise their hand and share the love! You are only as strong as your weakest game face. So put on your best one!

Once you've given this list a gander and you start your planning you will probably feel a bit more at ease as you enter into your classroom. Remember that a perfectly curated room will not make a great teacher. It's about the planning and thought you put into all the small decisions.

2

Respect Is Greater than Being Liked

How can I become the teacher my students need?

I think as teachers we can all agree that we (hopefully) joined the profession because we love children. With that in mind, we typically want them to love us back. We want to be like that teacher that we remember from our days in grade school. The one that inspired us to become a teacher, and that created for us the memories of what a good teacher is. I can remember being a kid and counting the days down for when class lists would be posted in hopes I would get the teacher I wanted. I hoped one day that I would be that teacher.

In my second year in the classroom, I was placed with a group of fourth grade students. I was so eager to be liked and be the "cool" teacher. In hindsight that really isn't something you can strive for, but more on that later. My rules were lax, and my grades were all fairly high. I just want every kid to be happy. When it came to tests, I made them all relatively simple and gave grace in the grades where maybe I shouldn't have. "Oh, I'm sure they meant to capitalize that letter," or "I mean they got the answer right, so maybe I won't mark off for not showing their math work."

With all of this relaxed style and desire to be liked it really came to no surprise that my kids were wild with a capital W. I would sit in my car in the afternoons on my long drive back to town crying and wondering why were they so crazy? How could I have gotten the loud and insane students? Again, this is a part of my teacher profession where some humble pie was in order, but what I failed to see at the time was my next tip.

Tip #2
Respect
Is Greater Than Being Liked

What I have found since that group of fourth graders were two things. One is my "don't mess with me" voice and the second is my "look." Every good educator knows the "look" the one your mom would give you when you were whining for a toy at the store, or your teacher looked at you when you were talking in a lesson. These two things would become the greatest management tools I've had in my skill set.

When I left that year in fourth, I really didn't feel like the kids liked my class. No matter how cute the décor was or even that we did fun activities such as putting on a class play I really felt like I had let that class down. I couldn't understand why though. I did all the cute stuff the senior teachers did, and I had tried so hard to be the fun teacher. Why didn't those kids like me? What I learned is this: If being loved is your ultimate goal then being liked can't be in front of your mind.

I went into my third year with the knowledge that this class was going to be a bit…squirrelly. I knew I had to have my big girl pants on and ready to not mess around. Those first days I was super tough. We practiced lining up over and over again until it was quiet. I sent home notes to parents when behavior got a bit over the top, and I was a really tough teacher when it came to my expectations. Again, that little voice in my head said, "don't be too tough, or they'll hate this class." However, this time I told that voice to shut it. I needed to be a strong teacher, or my kids wouldn't learn all they could. I stood my ground and didn't waver and expected to get some negative feedback when it was all over.

However, what I found was the complete opposite experience as with my fourth grade class. My kids really loved their year in second grade. For years since that group left me, they have come back for hugs daily, and we have a much stronger relationship for it. Kids do not need you to be the cool teacher. They need you to be the teacher that cares for them so deeply, that you show them how to succeed. Yes, those kids tell others my class is tough. Heck, now I even tell my parents and kids that on the first day. The thing is though my expectations are incredibly high, and that tells those kids, "I believe that you can achieve this level of success."

You can have the cutest decor in the school. You can have class songs, STEM activities for days, and a behavior system with trinkets that make the kids jump for joy. However, if you don't have that firm hold of your behavior in your room, then none of that is going to matter. Kids thrive when they have clear boundaries, and consistent rules and consequences. Yes, of course, you need to show these with love and understanding, but without firm control on these the kids believe these guidelines don't exactly matter.

I had a student named Mark who was the epitome of a rabbit in a glass shop. I was on that student every few minutes. He would blurt, move around, and not complete his work if you let him. The rookie me would've just said, "that's just how he is, let him be." The new me wouldn't let him move an inch without me knowing about it. I constantly gave him love and positive affirmations, but I also was tough. I talked to his mom often, and I never budged for a minute on the rules. He still tells me constantly I was his favorite teacher. He knew I cared about him, and that is why I tried so hard to help him be his best self.

I learned that being tough is also being loving to your students because it shows them you really care. You can't let the mind of a child and their picture of you dictate every move. Remember, they are kids. You, my friend, are an adult. Spend those first weeks nailing out all of the rules and procedures. Content and cute activities can wait. It can be so tempting to move into the curriculum when you see your peers do, but only you can know your kids. Feel out the room, and if they are still lining up and whispering, then have them sit down and try again. I break up my first weeks with procedures and cute activities. This way I balance the tough with some fun as well. Practice walking in the hall and make it a game. Tell them you'll pick out a student at random and that student will be monitored as they walk. Then give a compliment to that student if they do well. Kids love praise more than a little trinket in the toy box that soon gets forgotten.

This isn't just about behavior though. This is also a rule that applies to grades. Now later on I will discuss more giving grace with grades, but I also need you to hear this. Not every child is an A student. You are doing your students zero favors if you dumb down their grades. Your level of expectation is their level of comprehension. Don't try to be cool and give everyone good grades, because you're setting them up for failure. Either on a state test or even the next year, when they get a low score, they will feel duped. They'll not only feel resentment for their new teacher but wonder why you gave them an A? Was that fake? Were you really a good teacher? Their parents for sure will wonder about this as well.

When you give them a tough test or a tough assignment, you are saying, "I believe you are smart enough to overcome this obstacle." Don't shrink yourself and your ability to teach them the hard stuff because you want the happiness you believe comes with that A. That isn't where you'll find respect or love from your class.

If you want to be the teacher kids remember, and the one they are excited to have for their new class then you have to earn their respect. My students may not like me all the time. There are days I'm sure they are happy to leave me at the door at the end of the day. However, I have learned how to earn my kid's respect and that has made teaching a whole different game. When you have students that respect you, they will soon also love you, which is a much stronger feeling than being liked.

The How-To Gaining Their Respect

So, here is the thing that I love about kids. They are easy to be around, but man can they smell a fake a mile away. My principal told me once, "it's easy to look like you love kids for about a week, then it all falls apart once the honeymoon is over." As teachers we got to earn their respect not only by holding them accountable but by showing it consistently throughout the year. So how do I do that? Here are some sure-fire ways I've been able to keep my kids in line but feeling loved through the years.

2.1 Say Hello!

Imagine you're at a party, and it's filled with about 20 people all doing their own thing. You walk in and sit on the couch in the center of the room. No one looks up, no one says hello, and now think about how you'd feel? My social anxiety-ridden self would be incredibly uncomfortable. As someone who struggles with pushing themselves out there, I need that friend to greet me at the door and walk me in. So why wouldn't we imagine the same for our students?

In my fifth year in the classroom, I began to consistently greet my students at the door. I'd always sort of done this, but that year I told myself I don't care if it's cold, raining, or I need to write an email, I will not leave the doorway. I should probably mention the door opens to the outside, and so the weather is in fact an issue.

I had those cute five options for greetings at my door where students could choose to either greet me with a hug, high five, pinky hug, handshake, or a little dance. I wondered how this would affect my relationship with my students, and man was I blown away by the difference? That simple five to ten minutes standing by my door set up smiles and success for the day. My kids took that act as I cared about seeing them more than I did my own comfort or work. You may think you have students who believe that they are "too cool" for this. Those will be your high fives and handshakes, but a simple hello goes such a long way in creating a positive rapport with your students.

2.2 Positive Notes

We know that compliments on report cards are a must. Honestly, I see that as a requirement for us teachers, but how often do you put compliments into written word for your students? The best thing you can do is write a note when you are not expected to. One of my favorite things to do in the Fall is write a card for each kid during a random week. Nothing about that week is special, and so it's not anticipated. I write in the card a quote selected for each child and write what I think about them is awesome. Each card is unique to the point that if they compared them (which they will) they would barely see any similarities. That time given to writing those cards makes a lasting impact on the effect you'll see in your students.

I remember my first years, and I remember saying positive words of affirmation. However, I don't remember if I ever slowed down to ever truly write it out beyond report card time. That lack of sharing those thoughts with those kids leaves it open to the interpretation of how I felt about them. There cannot be a question about how you feel about your students or they will assume the worst.

I don't say this to be a negative Nancy. I share this because I genuinely have seen the changes from those few scraps of paper and comments, and it's something that younger me would've marked off as taking too much time. That the activity planning I was doing was WAY more important, and that just isn't the case. I have in this book a list of positive note ideas, and a list of compliments you can use to help put into words what you feel for your kiddos. I know that sometimes finding 24 different ways to say "you're awesome" can be a little daunting, and so I hope this helps get your brain working. Take the time to write a word on their desk in a dry erase marker or a note to send home for them to read. They will get so much more out of that than all the treasure box items combined.

2.3 Parents Are Key!

When it comes down to wanting to find a treasure trove on how your students tick the best resource you have is the parent. You can ask your fellow teacher about them, look at files, and guess during those first weeks. However, when it comes down to it asking the parent is the best route. I had mentioned before even starting to decorate and prepare your room to consider parent communication early on. However, even better is to add them to your team before the first-day bell even rings.

My favorite activity, and included in this book, is the parent homework letter. On the day supplies are dropped off parents are given a letter that asks them to write to me telling me about their child's strength, weakness, what concerns they have, and their dreams for their child in second grade. These letters not only give me invaluable information and get me excited for the new year, but also show the parent that you truly care about their child and their input.

When a parent appreciates you as the teacher and respects you, their child will do the same. When a parent doesn't particularly agree with you and isn't a fan, the child may also do the same. Your students are heavily influenced by their parents, which only makes sense, and so if you want your students to respect you then you need to have the parents respect as well.

I say this as a reminder to keep in the back of your head. Your days can get hectic and the workload that you have on your plate can seem overwhelming at times. However, make sure to answer parent's communication promptly and professionally. If you disagree with a parent, make sure you have the data to back it up. Always make sure you keep their feelings into account when making a decision. I am not saying you need to kiss their butt, though honestly, I kind of am, I am saying the parents of your students are more of your boss than the principal. Try to treat them with respect, understanding, and empathy.

2.4 Get off Your Phone

Honestly this is just a little blurb because sometimes we just need to hear it. In my third year in the classroom, I had a student write in her journal, "I love Mrs. McKinney because she plays with us at recess and doesn't sit on her phone." Ouch! It made my heartache that these tiny seven-year-olds could pick up on something so simple as what their teacher was doing at recess, but they can. This just acted as a quick reminder that remember little eyes are always on you, and where your attention is given is what they feel you value. So, make sure that it is them.

2.5 Be Tough Even on the Well-Behaved Kids

I can guarantee you will have that student that makes you want to pull your hair out. There will be the kid that tests your patience, and then there will be the other kids. The ones that are quiet and do their work. They seem to follow the rules to a T. You never have to send notes home to their parents, and you wish your class had just a few more like them. In the middle of the year your student, let's call her Eliana, who has been perfect all year begins to talk in class. You give her a quick look but move on because she's usually on her A-game. Who cares if she's just having a little slip-up? John (your talker) is always the one to watch, and so you ignore it.

Two weeks later you begin to notice a change in your student Eliana and now it's trickling into the other "well behaved," students. They are talking more, not giving their best work, and seem to just be a bit off. You wonder where did you go wrong? I have been there many times and I'm willing to bet the veteran teachers reading also have kids popping into their minds eye. Kids love to test boundaries, and so when you even let a little moment slide you are opening up a Pandora's box of problems.

Students need to know that they can't toe the line. Even the ones who rarely edge even close. I tell my students' parents at the beginning of the year, "At some point this year your child may have a week where they don't try as hard or maybe even tell a fib. It happens to all of them so don't panic or be surprised when it does." It's easy to let the ones always following the rules slide by when they make a minor misstep but don't! Every wiggle you give lets them know that it is okay, and that leads to more edging and mistakes. You have to stay firms and even if John is breaking rules left and right, it may mean even more when your others rebel. Don't give in to any students toeing the line. Once they see that you will give, you've lost a great deal of your power as a teacher and their respect as well.

2.6 It's Not about You

In a room full of students, it's easy to forget that each is unique. That some love to play sports, some love theatre, some may love art, and others may just want to read. When designing projects, activities, field trips, and lessons make sure to look at the group as a whole. I'm a former theatre gal, but in my fourth year, my kids were NOT into the presenting type of projects. I knew that I had to tone those down a bit. Notice I didn't give them up entirely, because students need to constantly learn new skills. However, I can't force projects and lessons that don't fit the type of learners I have. That just seems like I am making them do stuff because I enjoy it, and no kid enjoys that.

My fourth graders, for example, collectively did not like to color. I know crazy right? However, Miss Baggett LOVED to color. I wanted coloring in science, writing with illustrations, projects, etc. I put a little bit of coloring into everything, and you know what? They absolutely hated it. It wasn't fair to them to force my interests on them in their lessons. I even had a kid mention that maybe I should go to kindergarten where they truly love the coloring thing. This was the moment I realized that maybe older kids weren't for me.

We have to remember that at the end of the year it's their own experience (hopefully) in that grade level. We can't create projects and lessons that are based on solely our interests. That seems like a "duh" type of statement, but when you are scrolling through Pinterest are you making sure to think about what they would enjoy? I always have to sit back and consider that. When kids feel like you are taking their passions into consideration then they are more likely to give you the results you seek.

2.7 Remember Who Made the Mess

This lesson is a tough one sometimes and can be forgotten in the heat of the moment. When you have those times that a student pushes you to the edge, you need to remember a few things:

1. They are a kid, and they are obligated to make silly choices.
2. You are working and sometimes can be more stressed and wrung out, and therefore more prone to frustration.
3. It isn't the whole class who made their decision.

Number three I cannot say enough. When you have one to a few students who really set the ball rolling it's easy to give consequences that affect everyone. For example, limiting recess, putting away a class toy or reward, or spiraling into a lecture. When that happens, you are losing control of yourself and your class. The kids will resent you way more than be angry at their peers. They will see it as unfair and unkind, and then you've just lost a whole lot of ground with them.

When these moments happen, I strongly suggest pulling the student aside. Talk to them in a firm but low tone and find whatever aids you in calming down. If you need a moment to recuperate then take it. Do not under any circumstances punish the whole class for a minority's choice. It seems like such a simple hint, but I've seen it happen so many times, and have done it myself. Remember who made the mess in the situation and find a kind way to help them (and only them) clean it up.

Respect, in my opinion, is the greatest human emotion you can gain from another human being. Everyone may not love you, but you can be respected by many. When your students have that respect for you the ebb and flow of your classroom shifts. It becomes more of a team effort. I think of any sports movie where the coach earns that trust and loyalty from their team. That is when they begin winning the games.

3

Content over Cute

Where is the line between cute and content?

There is one resource that we teachers love, and I've spent probably thousands of dollars there over the years (sorry to my husband Blake) and that is Teachers Pay Teachers. If you have not found yourself perusing over the cute task cards and games, then I strongly suggest you grab a coffee and sit down and look it over.

When I found my way to this wonderful site a few years ago, and eventually found my favorite sellers, my teacher game greatly increased. Gone were the basic worksheets, and hello were the interactive games in centers. It really can be an investment that helps grow your classroom. I would say spend your money on a really great unit from there rather than a poster for your room. Now that I've set the stage of where cuteness can come from, I have an example of where this can go wrong.

In one of my first years, I really wanted the items I used to teach to be all appealing. I downloaded activity after activity from the site. Who needs a textbook when you have this cute passage on puppies? Why use that curriculum-based math activity when I can use this problem-based learning project instead? I saw the veteran teachers doing all of these amazing lessons and activities and I wanted to do them too! I wanted to start my career running with the big dogs, and not listlessly combing over my teacher editions. Plus, it's way more fun to look through cute worksheets than a textbook right?

I had a class that was an inclusion room with plenty of students in RTI and ESE, and who were struggling with learning. I had students that were years below their reading level and were required to take our state testing in the Spring. Many educators have been in that trench themselves. We are expected to get these students to the level of their peers no matter their ability level. However, my mind wasn't as much on these learning gains as they were on the cute egg drop, we could do in science. I became so focused on the cute learning possibilities that I didn't stop to ask…were my students actually learning? The reality was they weren't. They were certainly having fun with all of the activities, but the educational piece just wasn't there.

Just like tip two on the respect I was again focused on their enjoyment and that they were being entertained. If you were to walk into my room, you'd see the collaborative groups and the great activities. I even scored really high on my observations that year, but when the state test came my kids bombed it. I mean REALLY didn't do well. Part of me wasn't surprised like I said I had a lower class, but I didn't expect them to do that poorly. It was a blow to my ego, and made me wonder where had I gone wrong? I did the fun and engaging activities like everyone else?

Similar to earlier I had compared again to my coworkers and assumed if my kids were enjoying my class and I was being "innovative," that automatically meant that I was teaching well. That was what was being pushed in our school, and so since I felt I had met that requirement I thought I was doing a good job. There have been many times from parents since then that I have heard that they have disliked the classes their child's been in that was just what they called, "fluff," and that while they loved that their child enjoyed school they did not enjoy the fact that their child wasn't learning as much as they hoped.

So how do we as educators know when we are crossing over the line from having a truly engaging and thought-provoking lesson into the fluff category? Whether new or having been around the block a few times how do we know we are doing the best educationally for our students? The best thing we can remember as educators is my text tip:

Tip #3
Content
Over
Cute

Now don't get me wrong, I am not saying to not grab those fun and engaging resources. What I am saying though is really take a moment to reflect on the skills you are teaching. Are you explicitly teaching your kids the skill before you pull out the resource? I know that textbooks are not always our favorite thing. Hopefully one day there will be a curriculum that we teachers actually like. However, they are a great backbone for those first years in the classroom. Especially as you first start out, I suggest taking those and pairing fun activities with the book. This way you know you are actually teaching all of the required standards.

The reality of teaching is, not every activity should be cute. Yes, your kids may have resources that don't wow when you look at them straight on, but it matters more if it's teaching the child. Not all resources are created equally, and some simply don't really teach the content. I hate to say it, but there is nothing more obvious than when a student comes in who hasn't actually been taught the information, but maybe not even how to be an independent learner. You don't need state testing to get a feel for where they have been the year prior.

In my fourth grade group I had a wild child that came from a class that was notoriously never "actually" learning anything at all and the behavior was certainly leaving something to be desired. When I compared him to the two students I had from a separate teacher, who had been taught well and had a strong behavior plan in place, the difference was night and day. Yes, some students can be a little wilder than others, but it also is easy to see how they were trained the year before. I always keep this in mind when I am planning and working with my current bunch. What will these students say about me as an educator with their actions and ability when they get into the next class? They can say that I am super fun and nice! However, if their ability level and behavior show that they did nothing, then I have failed as an educator.

So, everything I research, select, and implement as a teacher I want to be the best that I can give. I want them to achieve their highest level of learning. The further you get into education, the more your mentors and veteran teachers will say that time in the school year is fleeting. What you are able to do in 180 days will shock you, but it will also make you feel like you are losing sand through your fingers. It's the craziest time warp you've ever seen! When it comes to figuring out what you're going to do you have to plan that time with a purpose and say hello to elevated content!

The How-To Planning With A Purpose

Take any data you can get after teaching a lesson or unit and see what is working and what isn't. It can take some time to figure out how to know where to spend your money when it comes to sites such as Teachers Pay Teachers, but really looking into each purchase can not only save you money, but also help you make wise investments in your curriculum. I have a few questions that I look at when it comes to asking: to buy or not to buy?

Go through this checklist and I would save if it meets at least four of the categories with a yes than add it to that cart!

TPT Check List

	Yes!	*Eh, Sometimes*	*Nope*
Does it cover the standards in your state? Some states follow different standard's, so this is important			
Is there an end goal or it is just fluff?			
Will this enhance your students' experience?			
Is it practical? Example: A multiple hour worksheet packet isn't always the best investment of your student's time			
Do you have the time to prep for this activity?			
Do you have the materials to make it work? Example: Buying a massive packet for morning work, but you only have so many copies or paper that you can use a month.			
Do you trust the seller? Example: I trust anything from Amy Lemons			
Does it do one of the following:			

- Reteach
- Enrich
- Complement the material your teaching

I love every teacher that has put materials on Teachers Pay Teachers. That is the amazing choice an educator has made to share their knowledge with the world and to do so bravely. Why I have this checklist is because I would spend even more money if I could. This isn't just on Teachers Pay Teachers, but also on sites such as Really Good Stuff. However, not all materials and cute items actually fit what we need for our students or currently in the classroom. Some things also are just made for cuteness, and sometimes we just don't have the time to do those things. Making a mental note every time you enter that virtual check outline can certainly help!

This may take some time as you learn what resources you actually would benefit from, and which are just simply cute. Where you can really apply those resources are enrichment, reteaching, and scaffolding your lessons to some really great problem-based learning projects. There are a few examples from over the years wherein different subjects the content showed to be more powerful than the beautiful image.

A favorite project I have done for years now in science is the Zoo Project. It's a form of a wax museum, but with animals. If you aren't aware of what a wax museum is, it's where students stand frozen in place, and when you press a button in their "exhibit" they come to life and share a short report on research they've done. My current students are second graders, and we literally take the whole year learning the skills to eventually do this project. I did a wax museum project in my first class too, but the difference in the outcomes is very different. Since I didn't really grow their skills in writing, research, and public speaking with that first group, the museum really fell flat. A cute idea, but with little content and skills to make it pop.

Now for the project with the zoo, I spent a ton of time teaching the skills. I help them learn to write strong essays, how to find text evidence so their research is strong, and we practice presentations all year. So now, even though they are two years younger, their presentations are phenomenal and are strong in content and are adorable. It has made a huge difference in the enjoyment I feel when they present, and I usually get a little teary because I see all that they learned in the year. It really has made a difference in the experience me, their parents, and the students feel. It is now a big accomplishment when they complete this massive project.

Another project that I am willing to bet a majority of teachers know about the project Flat Stanley. Based off the children's book most classes will have a small person they print out and then send it off somewhere into the world to have an "adventure." An adorable project that some use for social studies, and yet it can be incredibly surface level if not thoroughly done with actual education in mind. I used to do this project and left it as simple as it was done when I was in school.

I had my students send off their Flat Stanley's and that was that. No real research was done, just a fun activity to wrap up our novel study. Now first off, I'm not saying you have to make everything a dramatic lesson. However, when learning is mixed in with these fun activities it makes it all that much more enjoyable. After a year or so of very surface leveled projects I decided to add in some research. I had the kids look up information about where their Stanley went to. They had to learn the state bird, climate, state flower, song, etc. They had to use their creative writing skills to write a narrative of where he went and what he encountered. It was a multi-page project that could be in a book, binder, or poster. The excitement for the project grew the more they looked into their research. Some even would bring back a souvenir. I had a Flat Stanley return from Aruba with mini coin bags for everyone!

It wasn't so much about how grand the projects became, but the level of investment the kids took with what originally was a simple picture project. They still to this day know what the state bird of their Stanley's travel was and the idea of planning where one may take a vacation. It went from the end of a unit project to one of the highlights of the year.

Honestly, it's wonderful to sit back and think of each subject area and consider your why for each one. For example, journals, this is a task that so many of us use in our classroom. How are you using your journals? Are you using them for morning work, centers, or a quick homework piece? This is another area that sometimes we just do them because we always have, and the idea of an actual lesson coming from them can be somewhat ignored. I would just read them and write a comment back from time to time that went with what they wrote. I was so happy to just keep up with that relationship piece, and while now I still do that, I tried to tie more learning into it. This past year I would start with my response beginning with a comment on what grammar skill they could improve upon, how they could elaborate, or asking for more "strong adjectives" in their writing. A simple adjustment can make anything a bit stronger on the actual learning front.

From math games, to experiments, and centers always ask yourself the why. Why are you doing that certain activity? It is because they are actually learning, or because you feel like you have to because it looks good and is cute? I think that in education sometimes we are getting more and more lost in the bright colors and losing some of the actual educational components.

I hope this is taken as lovingly as it is intended. You do not have to rise to the level of your coworkers when you first start out. You do not have to make every lesson and activity performance for your students. There will be lessons that fall flat, and they won't meet their expected level of performance. That is okay. We have to continually be brutal and honest with ourselves. Sometimes when our kids aren't making the learning gains, we feel they should be, then we have to sit back and wonder if we are assigning the right things. We are teachers. We are meant to educate our students, not only entertain them.

Take your textbook, learn the standards, and evaluate what you want to use and where you need to pull from. Then go and find that resource that truly will help your students understand the content. Sort of like walking in Target, go into it with a plan of what you need to find, and maybe you won't buy too many unnecessary things. It takes years to accumulate all of the fun ideas for your teaching and to use them wisely. Each year find another project, room transformation, or technique you want to add. Then you can make sure to use it with content that helps your students really understand the subject matter. Make sure that content comes first, and then make it as cute as you'd like.

4

Destroy the Small-Group "Scaries"

Do small groups have to be scary?

In my first years of teaching I would hear time and time again that we must do small group. I so firmly believed that and still do, and yet, I didn't have much in the way of small groups going on consistently. The idea honestly stressed me out. I remember in my first class having the reading coach come in and show me how to facilitate a small group with the Tyner curriculum (phonics). I nodded and felt like yes, this is easy! I was eager to tackle small groups the next day and thought I would have it down pat. I bet you can, based this far into the book, guess how it went. Terribly!

My kids were absolutely insane, and I felt like my instruction at the teacher table kept getting interrupted and add in the wild behavior that went on even when principal was in the room and it was a fiasco. I genuinely had a student crawling on tops of the table growling at other kids, and one that climbs to the top of a bookcase yelling you can't get me. It was absolute crazy town! I felt like it was all just too much and that whole group must be easier, and thus I went straight back to the safety zone of whole group teaching and didn't budge.

In fourth grade it was better behavior wise, but I still felt like the instruction I was giving wasn't ideal. I was overwhelmed in the making sure they were doing their work and trying to implement the small group curriculum the school wanted to use.

I felt like I was in such a messy array of what exactly was supposed to happen that after several months I again went back to whole group instruction. This time I blamed it on prepping for the state exams.

However, I knew that whole group instruction wasn't the best way to teach. Differentiation during a whole group lesson is tough, and it made working with leveled text nearly impossible. I would watch all the videos, read every book on center rotations, and ask my coworkers what they were doing. I felt like small group instruction was tough, because I just didn't want to let go of any control. I was getting not only in my own way, but I was letting fear of getting out of my comfort zone stop me from doing what was needed in my classroom. I had a fear and so for some it may happen for them as well.

Tip #4
Destroy
The
Small-Group
"Scaries"

Whether you are just starting out, or just have yet to venture into the small group scene I'm here to tell you small groups are not so scary! If you are completely fine and have this portion of your teaching down pat then send positive wishes to those with the scaries! I truly believe those of us that struggle with small groups are my Type A and OCD friends. That is me to a T! We love being in control, and small groups are releasing a bit more control than you would in a whole group. So that can be really tough if that goes against your personality type.

For those of you lying to yourself, I've been there too, saying I'm really doing such a great job with whole group! You are limiting your own potential as well as the potential of your students. I am sorry to burst your bubble! I say it with love, because

I genuinely believed that I was doing great too. I was actually! My students were making their years' worth of gains! However, once I implemented small groups that group to nearly a year and half's worth! Not only that, but their maturity and independence grew tenfold as well. They were able to go into third grade with a strength that they'd just not gained when it was whole group.

Also, I actually enjoyed the day more and we got so much more accomplished. The kids all year would get so excited for centers, and when they were over, they always commented how fast they'd gone. If small groups are done well with intentional work, then they are enjoyable and fun. You are going to have to figure out what works for you when it comes to your small group rotations.

The How-To
Slay
Your
Scaries!

4.1 There Isn't a Perfect Outline

I will go ahead and tell you that no one has done centers perfectly. There are a million wonderful mentors out there you can follow and meticulously copy, but their kids are not your kids. My greatest mistake was trying to copy others and do my centers their way. That was incredibly frustrating, because sometimes that just doesn't work when it comes to your class. I didn't like the phonics program selected for my first year, and so it's of no surprise it didn't flow with me. However, by making sure I check that content we talked about I could go and find a phonics program that matched the way that I taught, and then I actually enjoyed teaching it!

Someone can tell you how many rotations you should have such as the Daily 5 or how many kids you have in a group.

I finally figured this out, it is better to have three strong stations than five and two be flimsy at best. Don't try to put more out there for centers if the content is not going to be strong. That is an incredibly huge mistake, because I can promise that will be the center your students goof off at. However, whatever centers you use in your classroom make sure they are all on the same level of importance and are equally as educational.

Do not compare your centers to someone else's. Your coworker may have them building letters out of clay or jumping out their syllables, but trust in what you know your kids need. There is not a winner for most creative center. So as you figure out what centers to use plan, work hard, and then trust that what you put out there for your students to do is going to make a difference in their education.

4.2 You Have to Pick Activities You Can Stick with

As I'd just mentioned there are some super cute center rotations out there. Even for the high school classes! However, do not implement a center that you cannot stick with. If you find adorable task cards on Teachers Pay Teachers, but you need to cut out six to eight copies of all of those cards each week, then you may want to sit back and think on that. I have bought so many cute task card kits over the years as well as games that I believed I would use. I honestly was excited to implement them into my classroom, and the content seemed strong and so I believed it was a slam dunk! Week one they were going great and I was excited. Week two I they were still doing well, but I was a little overwhelmed. By week three I was done, and my printer was tired and out of color ink.

It wasn't that the material wasn't fantastic, it was! I was just unable to keep up with it, and so they fell to the bottom of my teaching materials pile. If it's something that requires a ton of prep work or clean up don't overwhelm yourself with something you cannot keep up with or wait to prep them during breaks or summer months.

Centers can also be something that is reusable each day, such as building sight words with dough, using technology, writing in their journal, reading and response charts, writing on dry erase boards, and many other options. So, reusable doesn't mean it has to be boring, but it can save a bit of your sanity!

4.3 Technology Is You BFF

I will go ahead and preface with I do not have one to one technology in my classroom. However, when you can use technology it can make such a difference. There are two websites or applications that students can use that will do the grading for you, or at least make it easy to check!

The first and my favorite for classroom communication is Seesaw. I love this app because I can assign my students anything from an array of choices of activities in its library for free and created by other educators. This was a gem during remote learning. I can also have the students take pictures and videos on a classroom iPad and record their voice over it, label the picture, or even draw on it as well. Not only do I see the work and can comment back, but parents will see it as well, so it acts as a digital portfolio. On Teachers Pay Teachers you can grab digital sticks for that great grading to go option! Now I have proof of my students actually doing their work, and they can take turn with the technology while working.

Another favorite is using websites such as Prodigy for math (which is free) and IXL (which isn't). Both of these correct the students as they go so, they are forced to actually do the work, and I can look on my computer later to see what they did with their center time. I especially love IXL where I can track the questions they answer for ELA or math and see if they were working on the correct section.

If you have any ability to grab a device to use, then I suggest applying it to one of your centers. You don't need to change what you do in the technology center each day, and it will be that one center that's consistent and doesn't need much work on your end. However, you can rest easy knowing that their work is on task and rigorous.

4.4 Hang in There

I wish someone had told me this when I began teaching. It may take you days or even couple of weeks into beginning centers for your students to get the flow. The first weeks will in fact be filled with kids forgetting who group they are in, what center is what, how you do it, and how to transition. This is where type A people like me get super frustrated. However, soon the chaos will slow down and the kids will begin to sync into a rhythm. You have to hang in there until they reach that.

Anytime you change their groups or the stations they again will act like chickens who have lost their heads, but they will eventually find them. You have to be willing to wait out the madness to make it to the magic.

4.5 Make It Fun

Whatever you decide to do in your centers do not make them mind numbing. With the quick addition of highlighting, coloring, or manipulatives any activity can be transformed into fun. You just have to be willing to find those additions.

My kids will do anything to work with dry erase board. I don't know what it is about them, but they are like crack to a child when it comes to learning. We can simply be reviewing vocabulary words, but if I have them bring their white board, you'd think I invented the greatest thing ever! I store mini erasers in a toolbox behind my desk to use to count out syllables or sound out phonemes. I have erasers that are astronauts, French fries, sharks, and anything else you can imagine. When those come out during a very basic activity it becomes a whole new game. Even just letting them pick a highlighter color to use, within five seconds or I pick, is a way that gets them excited to highlight text evidence in the passage. Not all centers have to be complicated to be engaging.

Plus, it helps to find ways to let kids beyond your group know that you are watching them and for them to be on their best behavior. From time to time when each center changes I will pick a random student to watch. At the end of the center I will call their name and they get a prize if they were focusing during their whole station. I may have students applaud one particular group for their behavior in their center. I never go a day without acknowledging at least one student outside of my table, and one that is working with me. It's exciting for them to wait and see who gets praise and it reminds them that Mrs. McKinney is always watching!

4.6 Transition

The end of the center approaches and it's time to transition. There are many ways to do this, but yelling switch is not one of them. You can use any of the following to rotate centers.

◆ Give them 30 minutes of a song from your class play list. When the music stops, they need to be cleaned up and at the next center.
◆ Go on Amazon and buy a doorbell. When the bell rings it's type to go!
◆ Have a call out that signals it's time to switch. For example, I will yell in the tune of the cha cha slide, "Freeze!" and the kids yell back, "Everybody switch it up!"
◆ Flip the light switch and have them to the next center by the time the light comes back on.
◆ Have a timer on the Smart Board that shows them when it's time to switch.
◆ A simple bell will also work.

The key is having the kids move without a lot of fuss. If you can simplify it to a single noise or shout out, then you are going to have a lot less talking going on. Also, make sure that you've gone over how to transition so your students know what to expect. My students are asked to follow the three W's

◆ Whispering
◆ Walking
◆ Waiting to begin

Do not let your small group scaries keep you from achieving all that you can for your students when it comes to small groups. When they are separated by their reading levels and in a station addressing their needs their ability to grow is increased tenfold. Slay your scaries and start small grouping!

5

Stay Out of the Teacher's Lounge (Mentality)

How can I create a positive work environment?

When I was in college, I had a professor that said to us one day, "If I have a suggestion for your career in education it would be to stay out of the teacher's lounge. Nothing good can come from going and getting into the politics of it." Now as college students we just nodded and that was that. It's so funny how comments like that can stick in your brain for years, and then one day you realize exactly what was being said.

Now first let me say this. You by no means should hole yourself up in your classroom and become an educational hermit. You will not survive for many years in the classroom if you are alone. Life is not meant to be done in solitary, and especially in this career, you need to find your people. For me, I've been very blessed to be surrounded by fellow educators that have poured into me through the years, and this is especially true at the school where I currently reside. I have had coworkers at my wedding, and they've thrown me a baby shower. I couldn't do my job here if it wasn't for them. You need your educational tribe just as much as you need your curriculum. Now that I've gotten that out there, I do want to reflect on what I believe my professor meant with this comment.

Education can be a very political and competitive field. Depending on where you work you may find at times people are in an invisible gladiator match with their coworkers. This can be fueled by standardized test scores and Teacher of the Year award, and I've seen it tear apart some friendships. However, that humble pie is something we must constantly bite into time and time again and remember that we are here for the kids and not our own pride.

This lesson was one that I learned in an incredibly painful way for one year in my classroom. I had an assistant that had begun working with me, and personally I really liked her. She was funny, kind, and thoughtful. There was only one issue, and that was that she wasn't completely honest when it came to my kid's work. I would find assignments that had their answers changed, grades inflated, and content unlearned. When I asked a student why they changed their answers on a quiz they said, "because the teacher told us to." It even went as far as her hiding assignments from me when I asked to see them. So yes, it wasn't the perfect matchup, but I also failed to see maybe she was falling into a trap as I had mentioned before. Maybe it was more that she wanted them to like her than to give the grade they deserved. Whatever the reason, I should've sat and talked with her about it. I should've taken a bite of that humble pie and reflected on myself, was I really being a great coworker to her?

Now before I get into this next part, I want you to think about your phone, emails, or Facebook messages. Now really be honest with yourself, have you ever sent a message you shouldn't have about a coworker or friend? Let's be honest we've all had a moment where we said the wrong thing, and when we look at it in the black and white of the screen, we aren't too happy with ourselves. However, usually, those messages get forgotten and we move on. This wasn't the case in my story, and it was a lesson my friends and colleagues would soon learn.

One day in January after she'd been with me in my room for months, I noticed she was absent during our break. Then that afternoon I found she'd been pulled from my room, and she gave a harsh remark as she packed up her supplies. I stood there so puzzled and lost at what could've transpired. Within a few days I soon dreadfully learned what had taken place. I had let my students use my iPad for learning to help get more technology into their hands, but what I'd failed to do was turn off the iMessage portion. This meant any texts I had sent were visible when you clicked the button. Yes, this is a facepalm type situation, and absolutely mortifying. What I came to find was that she'd gone through every message on my device from when she arrived back in September. Any little thing was read and digested by her, and thus was one of the greatest mistakes I've made.

At first, I was so incredibly mad and hurt. How dare she scroll through my private messages with a fellow coworker? I can't believe my privacy was invaded in such a way! I really didn't say anything that I thought was terrible, but the reality was it didn't matter. When someone says anything about you, no matter how big or small it hurts. I was a coward and should've had those conversations about the grades to her personally. I fell into the awful habit of talking about her, and when you do that it really changes your heart and mind. Honestly, no one deserves it and if I could go back and have that conversation with her I would. We no longer are at the same school. She left at the end of the year and is now teaching somewhere else. To her I have to say, I am truly sorry. This situation helped make me a much kinder person, and more aware of what I let into my heart and out of my mouth.

Here is the thing, I am aware this story makes me look like a real witch. I made a huge mistake, and I learned from it. Like they say, "don't throw stones at glass houses." When you make those mistakes then it calls for you to sit back and reflect, and then decide what you'd do differently. That's my next tip on the list:

Tip #5
Stay Out Of
The Teacher's Lounge (Mentally)

As I said earlier, having coworkers to talk to during those tough days is imperative. However, don't let yourself get into the drama and politics of the school. I always say to myself, "not my circus, not my monkeys." Another teacher's class is not your business. Now, if you ever find yourself in a situation as I had then taken this to heart, talk to the teacher first. I made the mistake of gossiping with others that she worked with to see if they had the same issues, and really it didn't matter if they did. I needed to worry about my students and their learning.

That year was one of the toughest years I have ever had. Even more so than the hair-pulling experience and rowdy class. I had a great group that year, but after the iPad incident, I couldn't get out of the hurt that I felt. Not only that, but I found out the same week as this happened that I was pregnant with our first child. For months I dreamed of potentially quitting and staying at home with her. In actuality, I was dreaming of running away from my problems. My husband talked me into trying it one more year and see if I really wanted to be a stay-at-home mom once my daughter got here. As the year drew closer to the end, my heart tugged at the thought of teaching the new group of students. So, I rallied and signed up for another year of teaching.

To my husband Blake, thank you for talking me into staying. The sting and drama of that experience are long over, and the joy of my students reinvigorated my love of the classroom and my job. I can't imagine the pain and sadness I would have felt if I let petty drama ruin my passion for teaching. Sometimes as teachers we get into our heads that we have to be superhuman. That we don't have feelings and aren't able to feel emotions beyond our students. That simply isn't true. I had a really hard time that year, but it was a mess of my own making.

Moments like these also call us to re-evaluate and self-reflect internally and ask are we the kind of person we call our students to be? If we ask our students to show positivity and kindness, then we have to show that as well. That can be easier said than done, but I will say since I focused on being, "the sunshine," and finding that person that I can trust to be my aid and mentor I haven't felt that pull to negativity since my experience.

The How-To
Be The
Sunshine!
& Find Your Mentor

A turning point for me was in 2019 when I was feeling huge and pregnant and in our local Junior League, I won the award called the Kendra Fendt Ray of Sunshine Award. This award is given to someone who is a positive influence and a joy to work and be around. This wasn't too far after the debacle in January, and so I got to thinking. How can I show as much positivity in the demands of work as I do in the community?

The key to being the most positive version of yourself is the obvious. It's literally deciding you want to be the most positive version of yourself. Get the stick out of your booty and get out of your own head. Over time the positivity I felt just came naturally. However, in teaching you can get super over tired and worn down, and so here are some ways to keep on shining.

5.1 It's All about Your Circle

I'm going to get more into your circle at work later, but this rings true at home as well. The people you surround yourself with are going to be the energy you put into the world. If you have negative relationships in your life outside of work, then you may find that negativity seeping into your job. If you have a relationship that doesn't value what you do, then you may not view your job with value.

That can seem really obvious, but it can happen almost sneakily into your life. Post college I had a group of friends I spent a good bit of time with. For them work was just that, work. So, getting up early, planning after school, and devoting any extra energy into teaching just weren't important. Due to that I didn't give the effort I could've because I was hanging out with them versus planning for lessons the next day. Not to say you should be a hermit, don't do that it's not fun, but when I surrounded myself with friends who valued their jobs then I found a Sunday afternoon became more about prepping for work and less about hitting the bars for brunch.

5.2 Good Morning!

Your mornings set you up for the rest of your day. For example, if a football player going into the Superbowl didn't stretch and warm up, how do you think that game is going to go? If you said embarrassingly bad, ding ding ding! You are the winner. How you start your workday is a huge indicator for the rest of the day. My first year into teaching I would listen to the rap station on the way to work. Yes, in my bright colored pineapple dress I was singing along to Trap Queen which now I slightly chuckle about. I'm not saying that the song isn't great, oh it is, but it was a super weird mindset to be in right as I was about to go teach first graders. When I switched the station so more of a positive and mellow kind of music in the morning, I found my brain ready to go! For you, you may need the hype of a good booty dancing song, for me it just didn't get me in the right head space. I have found little things over the years to add to my morning routine (even post baby) that make me positive and eager to get started such as:

◆ Listening to my positive only play list on the way to work.
◆ Making sure I have time to drink my coffee even if I have to wake up a bit earlier.
◆ Having my clothes ready to go, because I'm not fashion forward enough to figure it out the morning of.
◆ Reading my devotional in the mornings before school.
◆ Getting to school early so I can use the copier when no one is there.

- ◆ Finding some positive affirmation to start my day with.
- ◆ Listening to a good teacher podcast as I set up my room (I'll share some later).

These few things help me get ready to go and to open my door with a smile on my face. Find those things that set you up for success and stick to them! Eventually you'll have a routine down and feel more prepared for whatever craziness the kids throw at you.

5.3 Check Your Health

No, don't read that and think I'm about to tell you to go run a 5k. It's okay, you can breathe now, no one is forcing you to eat only spinach and be a triathlete. However, in these last years I do believe health is so important. Not just our physical health, but especially our mental health. Our jobs center on pouring into others, but sometimes as educators we tend to forget about filling up our own cup.

You are not too busy to take time for yourself and your health. I will be blunt and honest about that, because as a new mom and teacher I sometimes tell myself that BS too. When we do not take care of ourselves, we are setting ourselves up for burn out. Not only that but when you are running ragged you are going to potentially lash out to others for your own low fuel gage. You need to be honest with yourself and see where you need to give yourself some love and grace. From maybe taking a walk during a work phone call, resting your eyes for the first 20 minutes when you get home, or setting one night a week to go be with your nonwork buddies make sure that your well-being is always accounted for.

5.4 Kill Them with Kindness

An oldie but a goodie phrase and man has it gotten me out of some pickles in recent years because it works every time. While not at work I had a best friend, whose negativity was toxic in my life. She was emotionally and mentally abusive to me in many conversations, but I didn't want to be rude and stuck it out. I would find at work I was worn down from her constant messages and belittling, and thus my health wasn't in great shape. I felt like no matter what I answered her negative talks with when it came to have an actual discussion resulted in more hurt and belittling. You can of course say, "walk away," but sometimes that's just not possible and in work especially it isn't.

So, what I eventually found that has been incredibly effective is just to say positive in the face of negativity. This has worked when coworkers want to say something harsh about another as well. People just want to hear you be a negative Nancy with them, and so when you don't give them the satisfaction, they lose that power. Usually once I just say a positive thing back, she would back off, and that portion of the conversation is over. Now she no longer comes to me to complain and vent off her negativity.

Though it can be tempting to vent alongside that coworker about someone when they get on your last nerves its best just to walk about or say something kind. Even it's something as simple as, "I like her red shirt!" It may help shut down the conversation and keep you out of a potentially harry situation.

5.5 Checking in

Your best friends as a teacher are checking in on yourself and self-reflecting. You will do this in your lessons, and you should as well with your relationships with others. Ask yourself:

◆ Am I making their day better?
◆ What word would someone else use to describe me?
◆ How can I be a better friend or coworker?
◆ What is it that they may need from me?
◆ When's the last time I shared something kind with them?

When it's your best teacher pal that you're with these answers may come easily, but when it's that person down the hall that sticks to her room and you never talk to one another you might have a tougher time. You don't have to be Mother Theresa but take the moments to brighten someone's day everyone in a while. You have no idea what wonderful insight they might be able to share with you for your classroom. It also makes the school a much happier and exciting place to work in.

Now that we've talked about the warm and fuzzies, let's get real for a minute. You will not always get along with your coworkers. That is a fact. We are humans with different points of view, emotions, thought processes, and personalities. You do not have to be perfect and keep those moments of frustration and anger bottled up. However, you have a choice in what mentally you want to hold in your life and at work, and how you go about things to better set you up for a positive work environment.

However, before you go into a vent session (which we all have) take a moment and re-evaluate to whom/where you are venting. There are very few people I will speak to about my frustrations and hurt feelings. I suggest sticking with family, your partner, or a mentor when you have those days. At my school, Ms. McLeod is that person for me. She has been my mentor and friend since my arrival. I know when I have those tough days with parents and students, I can trust her to help me through it. She gives me great advice, lets me vent, and then it's done. The conversation is over, and it doesn't go beyond those four walls. Having a mentor in your school is invaluable and essential on the tough days. There are a few key things to look for when trying to find "your person."

5.6 Find Someone in Your School or In Education Who....

+ Is focused on their craft as an educator.
+ Pushes you to be a better educator as well.
+ The conversations you share are always geared more often in the positive light.
+ Is positive in their interaction with others.
+ Is willing to share their resources and knowledge with you.

You can typically find someone who may fit these categories in your school leading a team or a professional learning community. They may be the person sharing what they know at the faculty meeting. They don't have to have been in the field longer than you, sometimes the younger teachers know a whole heck of a lot. They will be someone that gets to know everyone, but you don't hear their name by the school watercooler. If there isn't someone at your school who fits that bill, then look at local workshops and conferences and connect with someone there. You never know where you may find the Tina Fey to your Amy Poehler.

5.7 A Final Tidbit I've Learned the Hard Way

Another thing is that remember what you put in print is forever. You can delete messages from your phone, throw away letters, or delete emails. However, writing is a two-way correspondence, and I have seen several times where thoughts put in black and white can come back to bite you. Let's say your friend at work and you are angry at a particular coworker or your boss. You vent a bit over text message in anger. It seems like such a harmless text, and no one is going to see it right? Well first off, I hope you learned from my iPad debacle, and second those messages could be shared years down the road.

The anger you had at that time will probably be gone in a day or two's time, but what is said in print lasts forever. I have seen several friends in other careers have what they said in the past come back to affect their current job. It's so painful, because you may not even remember what was said, but that honestly doesn't matter. No one can truly know what you mean when you say it over text or on paper. It can completely get taken out of context. When you have those feelings of frustration or anger, then I suggest calling the person you wish to speak to or talk to them in person. You may save yourself from a fairly awkward situation.

When all is said and done just remember, you are in your classroom to teach. This isn't about who's the best, what they are doing, or who wronged you in some way. If you spend your time focusing on drama, then you have stolen time from focusing on your students. None of it is really worth it, and if you step back from the gossiping and negativity you will also find you are much happier in your job. It's always best to stay in your lane. You don't have to be perfect, but you can at least be kind.

6

You Are Who You Plan with

Whom can I add to my teacher tribe?

I've always heard the saying, "look at your inner circle, and that is a reflection of yourself," and from time to time I would do just that. However, when it came to my job in teaching, I never really thought of it that way. I would just enjoy the camaraderie and friendships that I made. A group of us would plan together. To be quite honest of the hours we planned I would say very little of that was actually planning. Most of the time you'd find us talking about our days in the classroom, our lives outside of school, and about how much we'd spent on materials from Teachers Pay Teachers. I always had the greatest time planning with them.

However, when it came time to teach and plan out the week, I would find gaping holes in my plans. Spots where we had meant to discuss what we were going to do, but a topic on The Bachelor had started instead. So, we'd quickly print off a worksheet here or an activity there. Just enough to cover the standards and get through a difficult day in the classroom. I didn't think much of it. I was the newbie, and these were my mentors. I just followed the course, and even though something didn't feel right with me I didn't question it. Even when there would be days where my coworker would say, "hey let's get our kids together to watch this movie," I'd find some excuse in my mind of why that was okay. I mean sure the Ruby Bridges movie was educational, and so was this science episode. The kids are learning right?

Again, I know, like I have said before I really don't like looking back at this version of myself. I'm aware that we all have those days where the worksheet or video is necessary. When I was pregnant sometimes that was an essential. However, that's not what I mean by these statements. I'm talking about just really not sitting down with best practices and data and finding the best way to teach. I just went with the crowd and didn't rely on myself and my education to do my best work. I sit back and think on that year and want to yank myself into the hall and give myself an educational pep talk.

When the year ended, I went to my current job. The thing about the beach school that I teach in is that you are completely alone. You are your grade level, and there's no one to save you. Yes, you have amazing coworkers to bounce ideas off of, and to get information from, but at the end of the day it's all on you. You need to know your grades standards and skills better than anyone, because if they move on and the next teacher is wondering why they don't know their standards then they are going to look at you.

When I heard this my fears crept in and I wondered how I would handle the situation. I spent the summer researching second grade standards, pouring over resources and books on teaching, and planning my routines to a T. I didn't get to really meet with another teacher to discuss the curriculum or students until I started preplanning. Once the year began, I found that I was the most confident I had been in my career so far. I would meet with the other teachers on data and standards, and though we had fun, I would get a ton of work done. I rarely ever came in on a Monday without the entire week prepared ahead of me. I focused on data and strategies and loved the consistency of knowing what to do. As the years went on this only grew. Even as much as signing up for a training at the Ron Clark Academy and a virtual Get Your Teach on Conference. The more I worked, the more I loved my job, and then it hit me what had been so wrong with me is this:

Tip #6
You Are Who
You Plan with

Like I had mentioned in Chapter 5 with the teacher's lounge, your coworkers are your greatest ally. They can help you find new ways to serve that student who just isn't understanding the lesson. They can lift you up when a parent breaks your spirit just a bit. They can even be there to celebrate the accomplishments in your life and your career. The thing is though, just like exes who brought you down or friends who helped you get a little too crazy at the bar coworkers can also have that negative effect on you in teaching as well.

They can be a negative in the actual best practices of your room, or it can be on your mental well-being as well. When you find yourself in a room full of teachers who love what they do, the feeling is contagious. You automatically can feel lighter and have a spring in your shoes. When the teacher down the hall has created the coolest room transformation, you may find yourself pouring over new ideas. There is nothing more motivating than surrounding yourself with positive and hard-working people. That infectious feeling can lean over into your classroom. So, it's key to find your tribe as a teacher to best prepare for the year.

The thing is, if you are in a negative environment where you don't enjoy going each day look at who you are around. If the lessons you are planning together fall a bit flat then look into that as well. Are they lifting your spirits or are they bringing you down? You can ask this for yourself too, because honestly, we sometimes need a reality check as well. All of this can ring just as true in our day to day lives and us trying to find the best version of ourselves. We have two types of school friends as educators. The people we love to get happy hours with, and what I call our tribe. They are the ones you plan with, go to on a rough day, and are the largest influence on your actual teacher. So, when evaluating or searching for your "teacher tribe" there are a few important things to keep in mind.

1. Do they help me plan the lessons that engage and cultivate student learning?

This is tough because I love fun meetings where you are able to talk about life and the fun details of your favorite binge worthy Netflix shows. However, are you actually planning something for your class? Also do they talk you into actually doing the right kind of educational practices or are they more in the "watch a movie" category. These people are the drive of your educational power in the classroom.

Look at what they are doing in their classroom. Is that the type of experience you want in your own classroom? Now don't get your panties in a twist! I'm not saying be judgmental. That wouldn't be us being a ray of sunshine. However, we all have a vision for our rooms and when we are planning it's important to surround ourselves with a team that meets that vision. So, this is where that evaluation can come in handy to see if you would be in turn planning the same types of lessons.

Creating a classroom environment that engages your students and cultivates their learning isn't easy. It helps when you have a team to back you up!

2. Are they there to cheer me up on days I have a rough go with a student/parent/admin?

Grab the Kleenexes! You find you've had a parent chew you out over email or an administrator came in to observe you and you were not prepared. Any veteran teacher will tell you that this is going to happen a time or two during the year. Any job, even outside of teaching, is going to have moments of difficulty and a few tears. That is okay and completely expected. However, what makes all the difference is if you have a circle of teachers around you during those chaotic days.

Find the people in your school that you can go to when the going gets a bit rough. That are going to give you a hug, a pep talk, and help send you back out ready to go! The key being that they are going to be there for you and help get you out of the funk and back out there. Not letting you drag on the floor and dragging themselves there alongside you. They are also willing to let you have your moment of tears and frustration, and not make it a time about them.

You do not have to be best friends to meet this requirement. They may also not be the teacher that picks you up Starbucks on testing days. This is mostly about loving on one another as educators and being there for each other in the tough days.

3. Do they make me a happier and better teacher for my students?

In Chapter 5 we talked about trying to be the ray of sunshine for others at your school. To do that you need fuel to get through the work week, and friends are the best kind of fuel! If you are surrounded by teachers who no longer love the profession and are just there for the incredibly small paycheck then shine bright, but also look elsewhere for that positive energy boost!

Find the people that love their job and are on fire for education. Like I had mentioned it is so contagious and will make you more geared up for a day at work as well. Finding the go-getters and passionate teachers will give you more hope and excitement for your career as a whole!

Any one of these things can make them a strong mentor/coworker in your court, and if they are all three then hold on tight! If that isn't the case, then maybe consider how you fit them into your work life and go from there. When you put yourself in positive and hardworking company you can't lose.

For an additional reflection though here is a checklist that I have created, "Positive Points to Ponder." These are a few things to consider if your teammates do and based on the score you can self-reflect or hold tight!

Positive Points to Ponder

	Yes! (3 Points)	Eh, Sometimes (2 Points)	No Way! (1 Point)
Love teaching			
Lift others up			
Happy class			
Act as their own ray of sunshine			
Trustworthy			
Always learning & evolving			
Share their ideas with others			
Positive conversation			

20–24 Points: Hold Tight! They are a gem!

14–19 Points: They are great for conversation at the water-cooler, but maybe not for planning.

8–13 Points: Maybe these are best relationships set for a wave at the faculty meeting.

Now, what if you aren't in an environment with those sorts of teachers. That can be entirely possible, and even for me sometimes I really needed a second grade educator's perspective. This is where you have to look at the treasure trove of educators out there who have created communities and resources to help you grow as a teacher beyond the confines of you school.

The How-To
The Search For
Support

6.1 Podcasts

When it comes to podcasts there is nothing better than a great educational listen. There are a few that I suggest that have been a great aid to me. One is Teacher Me Teacher by Jacob Chastain. His podcast is probably my favorite to listen to. He brings on guest speakers each week, and he is a great interviewer. This is a staple for me, and one that I stay consistently subscribed too.

If you are short on time or your drive to work isn't very far then Ten Minute Teacher Podcast by Vicki Davis is a great listen as well. Her podcast is short and to the point, and great for those that struggle to listen to lengthier podcasts. I enjoy this podcast during a quick break while cutting out laminate.

6.2 Conferences

I dare you to find a time an educator is more hyped up than at a teacher conference. These experiences are wonderful because you are able to not only listen to great speakers but meet fellow educators from around the world who are as excited about education as you are! Going to a fantastic teacher conference should be at the top of your bucket list!

One that I have attended and highly suggest is Get You Teach On. This conference is filled with all of those educators that you follow and the sellers you buy from on Teachers Pay Teachers. The energy is contagious and fun. You will learn so many wonderful lessons from self-care to math games, and fun ways to motivate your students. The speakers are always evolving and changing so you can go many times, but the lessons are changing and always new and exciting.

6.3 Icons

You will find that there are educators out there that are essentially our teacher version of your favorite movie celebrity. These are the models of teaching that are great to learn and grow from and make becoming a better teacher even more fun. For each of us educators that is someone different, and it may take a while till you find that teacher, but for me that person is Ron Clark.

Ron Clark is my educational icon, and different experiences he uses in his school in Georgia called the Ron Clark Academy I use in my own classroom. I created teams, built a stage, and have his essential 55 rules hanging on my classroom bulletin board. For Christmas my in-laws even gave me a ticket to go tour his school and meet him and I literally cried. My sisters-in-law for sure think I am the biggest nerd of all time. If you've not heard of him, I highly suggest giving him a Google search, and watch the movie starring Matthew Perry (Chandler from Friends) called The Ron Clark Story. It's an amazing story!

However, go out and find that teacher role model that you inspire to be more like! I may not get to plan with Ron Clark, but by following his models and methods, I get to learn from him and plan with his skills in mind. That has greatly added to my teaching experience.

6.4 Books

Well of course I am going to mention books. Though you are reading one right now and are over halfway through! Way to go! There are some amazing books out there that I have to highlight for you to pick up next for your professional development library. These books are some of my favorite educational materials I've learned from.

Harry Wong's *First Days of School* is essentially the teacher must have in their toolbox. This book I have read every summer before school because the tips are wonderful, and every year I get something new from the material. From how to layout your classroom, how to prepare for school, and the stages of experience for educators this book is essentially the science textbook of education. Please do yourself a favorite and go grab it!

Another book I don't hear about often but I think is a great book to have on your shelf is the book *Chicken Soup for the Teachers Soul*. This book is a great read as you need book for those days that maybe you are feeling a bit deflated with education. The stories are uplifting tales from the classroom that I grab on the tough days when you need a little bit of sunshine. This book is one to pick up in preparation for the tough days.

Of course, there are the professional development books that help you become a better educator by learning new skills. There is the Daily 5 which helps with creating a successful literacy strategy in your classroom. *Teach Like a Pirate* which is a fun way to figure out new strategies to be an engaging educator. Finally, I read the book *What Great Teachers Do Differently* for a school wide professional development. This book is great in picking out how to tips to be more effective in the classroom. Honestly, going through Amazon or your local bookstore you can find a treasure trove of amazing professional development books that are worth a gander.

6.5 Social Media

I had to save the best for last, because this is where I get my best ideas and tips for the classroom. From Facebook groups to following teacher Instagram pages, there isn't a limit to what you can learn if you dive into social media. I am in a few teacher Facebook groups. Currently I am in Simply Skilled in Second and Lucky Little Learner's group. These have been invaluable for me, because when there is a question I have for my class I go on there and ask it.

I don't have other second grade teachers in my school to bounce ideas from, and when I ask on these pages, I get the viewpoints of dozens upon dozens of other educators. The wealth of knowledge available is astounding! If you've not looked into joining one of these groups, I highly suggest that you do. The people that you ended up doing more planning with might be on the other side of the country!

Finally, remember this, that you got your degree/certification for a reason. Not only for a passion to work with kids, but because hopefully you wanted to make a difference. You have ideas that are worth using and sharing with others. In those meetings sometimes I just didn't have the confidence to share my own ideas, because I thought they couldn't be good. So, I let myself down by just not pushing myself. You entered this field because you may have a certain skill that makes you fit into this career. Find it and become confident in it. Your confidence as a teacher is your greatest asset. You have great ideas so use them!

Remember You Should Have C.O.N.F.I.D.E.N.C.E Because You Have:

◆ **C**ertifications that you earned
◆ **O**pinions that make you unique.
◆ **N**eeds that your students have that you can meet.
◆ **F**resh perspective on learning that some may not have.
◆ **I**deas that are worth sharing
◆ **D**reams that you have the ability to achieve.
◆ **E**nergy that you can use to positively improve a child's day.
◆ **N**ecessary training to know exactly what to do.
◆ **C**reativity to come up with new ideas.
◆ **E**agerness to help your students do their best.

7

Grace over Grades

How can I show grace to my students, but stick to the demands of my goals as an educator?

In a world where state testing takes center stage in education, it can feel like grades and student achievement is the most important thing. We as teachers try as hard as we can to ready our students for the next grade and to meet all of the standards that it entails. This center focus has made education a whole new animal and can cause parents, teachers, and students a ton of newly added stress.

I mentioned earlier that in my second year of teaching I wanted to be the cool teacher, and as such, I was overly generous when it came to my grades with my students. So, when my students didn't excel in their skills that year, I took a hard left to the other end of the spectrum. I would scrutinize the numbers that came in and look for the flaws in their scores. Where could I do better? What am I missing? As I looked at scores and grades the faces behind the numbers would dissipate and I would just focus on the details. That's the scary thing about grades. They are based on numbers and very rarely do they seem based on the actual student.

It's easy to fall into the numbers trap. That's what the world focuses on when it comes to the classroom and our prowess as educators. So, when my kids made low grades, or the scores weren't high I would send them home without a thought. They'll have to just try harder, and I will have to do better. I've seen this not only in myself but across the board when it comes to education. We are told to consistently achieve this perfect score, and so we get lost in the process along the way. We become like robots in an assembly line of students attempting to spit out identical results for each kid. This mundane form of teaching is one that any educator worth their salt will tell you is morally wrong as well as impossible.

However, that's exactly what I did. I felt the pressure that if my students weren't making the grades and the gains then I ultimately was failing, and I was. I was failing them. Sometimes it just takes your own light bulb moment for you to snap out of the assembly line. Mine was when a student said they were dumb when they opened their folder of low scores and incomplete work. I quickly battled with the phrases, "No you aren't! You can do anything you set your mind to!" How many times do our mouths spit this verbal diarrhea of sorts to placate the student and our own concise?

However, this is where self-reflection comes in and it did so for me in the car. As I drove the long drive home that afternoon something in my heart said, "To you, they are grade, to them it's their level of intelligence." Ouch. When I send home those folders of low scores, I am brandishing that they aren't capable of it. Now, some kids are just actually lazy. That is a whole different situation. I am talking about your struggling learners here. How would you feel if every time you turned in your lesson plans to your administrator it came back with marks all over it? Maybe some of you have experienced this firsthand. After a while those marks become almost expected and the dread of turning in any work will consume you. You'll begin to believe you are not capable of writing lesson plans.

I had this situation during a reading endorsement course over the summer, and man was it a wakeup call to empathize with my kiddos? Those of us in the course would get our assignments back essentially ripped to shreds. I wasn't using enough strategies, I needed to read more on phonemic awareness, and the list of my failures in my assignments piled on. I would sit anxiously awaiting my grades to come out, and as a perfectionist this was even more dangerous. While I did end up with high marks in the class, I'll never forget our last Zoom meeting. The instructor asked us how we felt about the course. No one unmuted their screens. Finally, ding, a message came through. A teacher had written, "this course made me question my ability as a teacher, and that was a tough pill to take." I replied, as well with others, that we agreed with her statement.

The instructor apologized to us and said that in her grading of our assignments she may have come off a bit harsh. That was it though, and we moved onto the next course in our certification pathway. I thought after that we as adults had the ability to share these thoughts and ideas with our teacher. That we were even remotely asked in the fairness and pace of the class (which was the toughest I'd ever done), and then I remembered. Our kids don't have those luxuries.

At the end of the day, we are there to teach children. Sometimes in the hustle and bustle, we can forget that they are literally tiny humans. Everything that we send their way as far as comments and grades are taken to heart. You as their teacher are the greatest thing in the world. So, when it comes from you that they aren't doing great, it can really hurt. It was so easy though to forget that, and act as the machine that sometimes the educational system wants us to be. So, I knew after that moment that I needed to change what I was doing. I pulled out the self-reflection journal and thought what is it that I am missing? What can I do to make this not only better for my students, but still meet the goals we need to reach? Then it hit me I needed to remember this next tip:

Tip #7
Grace
Over
Grades

Now as I stated earlier, no you shouldn't give only A's to your students. The term grace means "courteous goodwill." So, it means that we can give a bit of wiggle room here and there. I've made a rule with myself on how to judge if I am being "graceful with my grading," to check in from time to time. However, I will first start off by saying this: your grading is limited to YOUR classroom; you do not control the grading style of other teachers and how they run their room.

That I know can be incredibly frustrating when students just don't stick with us forever. They do come to us from other classes and leave for other experiences with teachers. However, you need to focus only on the confines of how you grade within your room. I say this because grade is sort of a "hot button" when it comes to school life. Some will say that you should grade very little as it stunts their creativity. Others will tell you to be tough, so they rise to the occasion. You'll have educators who give A's to all and some that rarely give A's. So, the grace first has to be with yourself and also to other educators.

There have been times over the years I haven't not wholly agreed with others on the grading front. This can be a source of tension in the work environment. This is where the "stay out of the teachers' lounge mentality" is paramount. That is for you administrator to decide on what is fair and valid in those student's education. This is where I follow the tips I mentioned earlier to keeping in my lane, and also realizing that they deserve that grace in grading that you are prepared to give your students. So how do we know if we are on the right track when it comes to grading?

The How-To
Grading
Gracefully

7.1 Keep It Average

This is my favorite rule to follow, because it has helped me get out of sticky situations with parents many times. Plus, it's a great way to constantly self-reflect on your teaching.

If the class average is less than 80% then I reteach the material or give them a second chance. I do not average the two grades. This is where I have to have a "my bad" moment and realize that it may be my fault as an educator that they didn't understand the content. That is sometimes humble to realize, but that is literally our job to do so.

However, if the average is above the 80% mark then the papers go home. No question about it, and when a student consistently falls below that, then some form of conference or intervention is in order. I do this in every subject and since implementing these rules I have had little to no issues with parents.

Now, we've all been there. Your student's parents send an email to meet with you, and they come in with guns blazing. They are ready to rip you apart and say that Billy is smarter than this grade that you gave. He is a perfect reader and an excellent mathematician. You must've just not taught the content correctly. That has happened to me as well. On Saturday (yes, a Saturday), I received the most hurtful message from a parent. That her child had never received below a B on an assignment, and what could I be doing that caused him to get a C? I literally cried all weekend and felt sick to my stomach. The beauty was though by following my 80% rule the parent didn't have the room to argue, because other students did learn the lesson and did well on the assignments. It was a fail-safe on me to check that I was being fair, and a check for the students and parents.

This has been my golden life raft for years, and a parent has a tough time arguing when you have data. Always have the data to back you up. If your class made below an average of 80% then why wouldn't the parent wonder what you did wrong? I'd already be wondering that myself. So, I have saved myself the embarrassment and hassle of some angry parent emails.

7.2 Stick to Your Mission

It's so easy to want to get lost in the numbers, but always remember your why for every lesson. Your district probably titles this as the objective, but I have it on my lesson plan as the why, which you can find in this book. Make sure that all the lessons that you are assigning and grading have an actual purpose to them. Parents and students can sniff out busy work a mile away.

This makes parents see red when they are given packets that do nothing for their child's actual learning. If you cannot give a concrete reason why you are assigning it, then you better not actually give it to your students. It takes away from their precious learning time and your time when it comes to grading. I have seen more worksheets go through the copier that are unnecessary than I care to count. There is fun, and then there is time fillers. Be mindful of what you are assigning.

I say this because it's unfair to grade an assignment with little to no purpose with a low grade. In that class I mentioned earlier we were given copious amounts of work to complete in the three-week period of the class. It was supposed to be a 60-hour class and man did she make it every bit of that 60 hours! I did so many assignments that at the end when she asked what was the best thing we learned I was honest and told her, " I mean I know a learned a lot of great stuff, there was just so much of it I can't remember it."

We do the same in our classrooms with busy work, and then wonder why our students can't remember what they learned that day. Do not give work just for the sake of having numbers in your grade book. Stick to your mission, which is giving your students a solid education with worthwhile learning opportunities.

7.3 Don't Grade It All

Your time is precious and so are the words you share with your students. So why waste them on every paper that comes to your desk? Students and their parents don't need every single little thing to be graded or marked. If anything, it takes away from the papers that genuinely do have the care taken to be thoroughly reviewed. Sometimes we even miss out on the opportunity to make marking students papers fun and a bit more enjoyable.

There are so many options when it comes to grading alternatives that they are worth considering the next time you have a stack of papers to send home:

◆ Stickers still remain supreme in the best grading alternative out there, and you can usually find some great ones at the Target Dollar Spot.

◆ Smiley faces and silly faces with flair pens and a bright touch.

◆ Use the compliments list in this book to find some alternative ways to share a thought and positive thought with your student.

◆ Use a check list to convey what skills were done well. I do this for writing vs giving them an actual grade.

◆ Give hold punches in a reward card for a job well done. Once the card is full, they get a treat!

◆ A simple ✔, ✔+, or ✔– will suffice at times.

◆ Have them peer edit each other's work to give each other feedback.

◆ Simply hang up on a board with the work that was "extra special," and help boost their confidence as well.

I always thought that sending home papers that weren't graded wasn't doing my best, but honestly, sometimes those little touches can brighten a child's day more than a 100%. Plus, you'll be less likely to pull your hair out. Give yourself some of your days back and give some leniency to your students.

7.4 Better to Raise the Bar

My biggest regret with grading would have to be more so when I used to give A's than when I gave the tougher grades. There is nothing more frustrating than when teachers give everyone the double thumbs up. This to me I've seen cause more tension that I ever see with the teachers that are tougher. Why, because the teachers who have to actually give the real grades become the bad guys. It's not only not fair but it's completely unrealistic.

I learned from that mistake and vow that is one I will never lapse back into. I would rather push my students to be the highest level of themselves possible. I tell my students' parents that students will rise to bar wherever you set it and so set it high. It's amazing what children can accomplish when that is the expectation for them.

However, it is also important to remember that a high bar doesn't mean above their ability level. While I may read books to my students that are a grade or two above their reading level, I don't give them grades that reflect that. The reason being that grades should simply reflect the standards of their current grade level and nothing above that. It's unfair to give grades for a standard that they aren't even required to learn just yet. Set them up for success and not extra stress!

7.5 Communicate Always

When you begin the year, you will have some sort of opportunity to present to your student's parents what your expectations and experiences are like within your classroom. Whether it is during this time or parent conferences you need to be completely honest with them about how you plan to grade their child's work. Giving them more information is better than less. Share with them the percentages of each portion of a subject and explain why some are higher than others. It's always better to give more information than less.

This is also a great opportunity to talk with them about what you believe their child is capable of. I go in that first "Meet the Teacher," telling my kids' parents that I am a tough but fun teacher. That I set a high standard for my class, but that my students always reach it. I go ahead and let them know what typically my students can do by the end of the year. So, when they start their first months in second the parents know exactly what is going to happen in my class.

Another great way to share your grading with parents is to have rubrics and check lists to share with them. I find that parents are a lot more willing to accept their child's grade when they can see where they lost points. Rubrics are so simple to make and look up, "rubric generator," on Google and you can create one for any lesson or project you so choose. By doing this you are opening the communication more with the parent on your reasonings behind that letter grade.

You don't have to bend to your student's parents will, but you do need to be firm in showing what you plan to do for their child. So, when their child struggles for the first time they aren't surprised and more willing to be on a team with you. Communication when it comes to grades is key and doesn't have to be a sore subject. Being up front and honest can create a positive relationship with you, the student, their parents, and academics as a whole.

Finally, there is nothing more beyond grading than showing the word grace in all we do when it comes to looking at our students' work. We have to be at the upmost, kind when it comes to what we say and do as we enter those grades into the grade book. So, we follow these adjectives to see if our hearts are not looking at numbers, but at the faces of our students.

- ◆ Generous
- ◆ Reliable
- ◆ Acceptable
- ◆ Compassion
- ◆ Empathy

Are you being a bit generous when it comes to how you are grading their assignments? Sometimes going the more generous route like giving a point to round numbers to the next letter grade is worth doing. Maybe not marking off every single lowercase letter in a name, but just the one to get the point across. Little decisions like this help you keep in mind the mental state of our students. Make sure that you are reliable. That you are someone that grades consistently the same way, and not based off a change of the mood or feeling. Is what you are assigning acceptable for their ability and grade level? This could be that you are assigning something too difficult or even too easy. Finally, do you have compassion and empathy for the work you see your students giving?

Remember this acronym as you grade that next large math exam or the research paper they recently turned in. Remind yourself that you have the power to make a child feel more confident, and that depends on the way that you check their work. We are not meant to please everyone with a smiley face and 100% on their papers, but the way that we do make the corrections on their work speaks volumes about the types of educators we are. So be graceful in grading and show your students that they are more than a number.

8

You Are More than Your Classroom

Who am I beyond the field of education?

There's always a funny moment for teachers when you are out shopping or at a local event and you see a student. They look at you like one would look at an animal at the zoo. Typically, my little students get super shy and say a brief hello. Only the next day in class brag how they saw Mrs. McKinney at the movies! In the movie *Mean Girls*, they even make a joke about seeing their math teacher in the mall and "how it's like seeing a dog walk on its hind legs." I always thought these jokes and reactions were so funny. Of course, teachers have lives outside of school! I couldn't imagine where these thoughts and opinions of our profession could come from until I remembered a point in my career where I was the literal butt of that joke.

I was coming up quickly upon my wedding during my second year of teaching. I sat down to write the guest list and plan events such as showers and my bachelorette party. After I got past the portion on college friends to invite, and my coworkers that I enjoyed, I suddenly realized a sad thought. In the two years since I'd moved home, I had really not put the effort in with friendships outside of the school. I'm not a super awkward person. I love to be involved in the town and to make new friends. I had just focused so much on my profession that I'd really not given the effort anywhere else. My time had been eaten up creating the life-size zoo or making the classroom look like an airplane. I spent evenings cutting laminate as I binge-watched Grey's Anatomy with my fiancé, and Fridays I passed out asleep before 8:00 after a long week. I felt so defeated and so much like a weird loser and I let that really get in my head. I would sit and think, "Maybe teaching is all I am. It's what I feel confident in, and who cares if I do anything else?" However, I found that I really did care. I wanted a life beyond those four walls. I wanted friends who I talked with about things beyond my students and last week's test.

After the wedding passed that summer I sat down and thought, I need to make a change. I signed up for a few local organizations to volunteer my time. I began a book club that brought strangers together, and we soon became friends. I put myself out there to make friends on apps like Bumble BFF and fellow bloggers in the community. I took time out of my room to really cultivate relationships with people who weren't teachers. I was suddenly surprised at how much more rejuvenated I was in my career when I stopped making it the center of my world. That's when I learned the oh so important lesson:

Tip #8
You Are More
Than Your Classroom

The more pressure we put on ourselves to perform and live and breathe the classroom life is the time we are going to easily burn ourselves out and leave the profession altogether. There are so many resources and strategies to get you out of the classroom with time to hit that gym class or happy hour afterward. You don't expect your students to live and breathe your class. You want them to make friends, enjoy an extracurricular activity, and enjoy some creative time with their family. So why aren't we doing the same for ourselves? Your mental health is the most important thing when it comes to you sticking it out a few years.

When you put these fun experiences and people you could meet off and stay in the school environment each day, you are missing out on opportunities to grow as a person. When I forced myself to step away from the desk and experience more in life, then I became a much better teacher. I was more well-rounded, energized, and able to bring new experiences into the classroom.

Here's the thing, hopefully, if you're reading this then teaching is your passion, and that's why you want to spend that time cutting laminate, searching through Teachers Pay Teachers, and finding new room transformations to try! However, when you conform yourself into a small bubble of types of people and experiences, then you miss the moments that can inspire great moments for your students.

By going out of my comfort zone to join new organizations and getting to know others I have added to my students' education and my toolbox as a teacher. Through the Junior League, I met a wonderful woman who runs our local Junior Achievement group, and now she's sent me volunteers for the last three years. I've had people donate items to my kids because they thought they might want it. We've had guest speakers, field trips, and more room transformations due to help from people I've met since I started getting to know others in the community. These people were able to pour into my students their talents, and thus create a fun experience for my students.

To do that you'll need time, and sometimes it just feels like we don't have any. Especially after having my daughter, I felt like I was battling the day for more hours to squeeze out. Then I just have to tell myself, "You are more than the person that educates tomorrow's leaders. You have a life that is worth living outside those four walls." That's when I set down the papers to grade and walk home ready to love on my daughter. So how can we as teachers set ourselves up to enjoy our lives and get the most out of the time we have?

The How-To
Get Your
Life Back

Now there were some practical things I did to make this possible. I spent fewer breaks chit-chatting with coworkers, and more time preparing materials for the next day. I spend one night a week to plan for the next week, usually Wednesday nights, and then make my copies on Thursday. So, when I leave on Friday I am prepared for the next week, and nothing goes home. I made getting organized a priority and took the time to make it so I can find items when I'm looking for them. I only add one big project or transformation per year to the ones I've already gotten figured out. It gives me something to look forward to, and I don't feel like I've bitten off more than I can chew.

Most importantly I realized I needed a bit of a lesson in time management. It wasn't something I realized I needed to evaluate until I did, and it helped me get the most out of the day, and to not waste so much energy on the wrong things. It's all about being aware that time is your most valuable resource and so we have to allocate it properly. So how as educators can we do that? How do we get it all done in the day with enough time to make it to happy hour?

8.1 Organization's Your New BFF

The greatest investment I have made over the years would have to be in anything that helps me keep my materials organized. I have in this book the Teacher's Guide to Sanity, but let's go over why organization is going to be so important. There is nothing that I dislike more than losing time trying to find the certain color Astrobright paper or throwing away papers I can use later. Once I realized I had certain learning materials I knew I would use in the years to come I stopped throwing away the original copy and kept them stored in neat hanging folders to grab the next year. It saved me having to reprint materials, which spared me time and saved a tree!

Not only do my drawers, bins, tubs, and organization habits help me save time, but it also helps my students. In the middle of centers, I'm not hearing students yell asking for where the lined paper or manipulatives are. I'm not wasting my group's time getting up to fetch a ruler or base ten block. Tiny moments of time that you spend searching through the mess of your classroom, or even your laptop folders, suck away the time you can allocate in other places.

Now I know that not everyone is a Marie Kondo of organization. It took me years to finally make the investment in my time and storage to get to where I am now. However, the mental sanity and time saving that it has given me is beyond worth it! So, take my guide and start saving yourself the headache of trying to find that right color paper.

8.2 Eliminate Distractions

Your Apple Watch buzzes, your phone lights up, heck even your Mac has little notifications popping up in the corner. How in the world are you supposed to get anything done? That's the thing you won't.

I'm like a magnet for the distractions of life and technology. Heck, even as I'm writing this my husband is walking back head banging to some music. I find that getting a moment's peace in my world is sometimes nearly impossible. Now notice what I said, "nearly impossible," meaning that it is doable. So how do we make that magical world of no distractions appear? So glad you asked!

First off you have to be honest about how much you are allowing distractions to come in. Are you honestly leaving your phone next to you, so you see it light up every time that a notification comes through? Do you have notifications programed to pop up on your laptop from Facebook? Are you answering every beep and vibrate that comes through on your phone? Then you are actively feeding the time sucker. We got to stop feeding into it.

Here's what I implore to you. Set aside a certain allotted amount of time a day to focus on your work and only that. Maybe it's just an hour after school. In that time, you will put your phone in your purse, maybe take the Apple Watch off (after you add in another hourly stand goal), and you log out of

Facebook. In that time, you are focused on only school. See how much you can accomplish in that hour.

Now another distraction can come bombarding into your room and that is your amazing coworkers. Let me share this gem with you. Have a time that your coworkers know you're MIA from the chit chat world. No one is going to care if you mention how much you plan to get done after school. It's an off-hand way of saying imagine my room doesn't exist today. I have to do that sometimes, because I hate passing on a post-school day talk comparing notes.

Your time is valuable, and so it's up to you to protect it.

8.3 Track Your Time

There is something I am terrible about, and it's realizing how much time is passing when I am in my classroom. It's like the Twilight Zone and time never seems to really exist when I'm in there. I will begin organizing my books, cutting out laminate, or planning lessons and suddenly it's been hours and time to get my daughter from daycare! That's the thing about teaching, we could give hours to our craft if we wanted to, and sometimes we really just want to. However, it is important to realize that we need to get out of our rooms after a certain point and go and live our lives.

I will be honest with you. There is really only so much time you should be spending in your classroom after school. I have long accepted that a teacher's to-do list is never actually done, and we always seem to add to it, and so we should be aware of that and get home to our families. However, if you are like me and you find yourself in the Twilight Zone, a timer is now your best friend.

When the day ends set a certain amount of time that you think is sufficient to be in your classroom and promise yourself you are leaving when it goes off. Make sure you are leaving at a time to go and do something that is beneficial for yourself. When the alarm goes off under no circumstance stay any longer. Go home! Your work will always be there; however, your kids, friendships, partner, and life won't. This is where we have to actively turn off the teacher mode and turn on your real-life persona.

8.4 Stop Aiming for Perfect

There's a word in the English language that I cannot stand and yet I struggle in trying to achieve it, perfect. I think there is something in us teachers engineered to strive for a level of perfection. For each of us it may be different. For some it may be the perfect looking classroom. For others maybe the perfectly curated lessons. Lastly, some may just want to be the perfectly fun and bright teacher. Some of us might be triply insane and want all three, which is where I feel myself sink into my chair knowing that's me.

When my mindset is on perfect that's where my time truly gets zapped. I will spend way too long on a project or decorating my room for a transformation. I swear the further into this career I get the worse it becomes because my ideas just won't stop! However, sometimes when I'm my most sane self I remember that all of this isn't for me. It's for my students, and my level of perfection when it comes to classroom décor really doesn't matter to a seven-year-old.

We have to be okay with the good, because that is what it is. Good! We measure ourselves against our toughest selves when in reality the judge really is only the eyes of a child, and they think everything is cool! So why are we so hard on ourselves? I truly believe we are jumping through the hoops to get the praise from someone else. It might be admin, a fellow coworker, or a person on social media who likes our post.

We are so focused on being admired sometimes as educators and meeting a level of perfection that just isn't attainable. At least it's not in a healthy way. This is what I want us to think about though, and it's tough for me. Which is better? To spend copious amounts of time on room transformations and décor that gets torn down, or spending time at home with loved ones. Now, don't get me wrong. I love a great room transformation and do several a year. However, since having my daughter I have realized that the same level of effect for my kids doesn't require nearly as much time as I used to give. I could spend an hour or two on a done-up room vs my usual multiple afternoons spent on it, and the result is still the same.

No offense. You are not perfect, and neither am I. We weren't made to be. Our students honestly prefer us when we are not, because that's when we show we are human. We have to give ourselves grace to give our students our all, but not set the bar so high that we get worn out climbing to it.

Don't waste your time trying to achieve something that doesn't exist.

8.5 Focus on the 20%

I recently heard of a cool study by Vilfredo Federico Damaso Pareto. He was an Italian born in 1848. Through observing his pea plants in his garden, I won't bore you with the details, he realized that 80% of results will come from just 20% of the action. This theory called Pareto's 80/20 Rule has been used in economics, health care, and now we are discussing it with education.

So, the idea is that you can do a whole slew of work, but 80% of what you reap from that work really only comes down to 20% of what you actually did. So, in teacher speak, let's say you use all of these amazing new strategies on a student in your class. You spent all this time learning and implementing them all. However, for all that work you did the gains the student made really was from only one or two of those strategies. While we have to do this sometimes to help find the way to reach a student this rule can apply to our time as well.

You can have a to-do list a mile long, but the reality is that only a few of those things are actually product and helpful to your students. So instead of wearing ourselves out trying to do 100%, we really need to analyze and figure out how to best figure in the 20%. The key to that is understanding, you can't do it all.

You don't need to sign up for all the committees in your school. You don't need to take on every project and volunteer for every school event. You have the power to say no and shorten what can sometimes be that ever-growing list sitting on your desk. Look at all the things you planned to do. Cross out all the "may dos," and only keep the "must dos." If you were honest with that your list should've gotten exponentially smaller, it should only be about 20% of what you just had on your plate. If not go back and really be honest and eliminate some more items.

For those that need to hear it. The world will not end if you don't join a committee. It won't end if you don't design the year-book or chaperone the school dance. Your school won't fall apart if you don't decorate your room for a holiday. When you stop placing all of these imaginary expectations on yourself the burden of education can become so much lighter! You can actually enjoy the few things you need to do versus drowning under all the things you thought you had to do.

It's time we stop saying yes to everything and live in the margins of the 20%. We need to find the things that are worth our time and our students' time and stick to those. Give what you can and live your life outside the margins.

So, what do I do with all of this free time?

So, this is the fun part. Sit down with a piece of paper, a Pinterest board, or magazines to cut apart and dream. You can even use the dream guide in the back of this book! Think of those things you imagined as a child that you wanted to do. Now's the time to make those dreams come true! What about books you wanted to read, movies you wanted to see, or places you wanted to travel? Take the time to plan those out and make them happen!

Have you taken the time to find your tribe yet? The people who can get you out of your educator comfort zone. If not, where can you join in your community to make those connections? Meet people who inspire you to achieve more than you believed possible! What's a hobby you've wanted to learn? This is the time to reflect and find who you are aside from your Mr./Mrs./Miss persona.

Then leave a little earlier each day to help make these dreams happen. Maybe leave ten minutes earlier and see if you are okay the next day. Then maybe stretch that to 20 minutes and see are you too stressed the following morning. Keep going until you find that limit where you know you are leaving and enjoying your life, but you aren't coming in like a hot mess the following morning. I'm a morning gal so I tend to allocate that time in the mornings, and still have plenty of sunshine to enjoy after the days are all done.

So, get out there teacher! Get your time to yourself and fill your heart with things that make you happy. Then go back in tomorrow refreshed and ready to enjoy time with your sweet students.

9

We Have to Be the
Game-Changers

*I want to change the world, but can I do more than just
beyond these four walls?*

If I were to pick a character trait, I think that all great educators have it would be the word, empathetic. We care, and that's
why we picked a job that can be extremely frustrating at times.
We have the power that most professions don't have, which is
to change the future. However, sometimes we let fear get in the
way of making the lasting impact we have the potential to make
as educators.

While there isn't one particular moment in my career that I
believe that defines this fear I believe it's made up of the little
moments where I didn't fight for what I believe in or share my
values with my students. It's the moments of movies that depict
homelessness where we didn't get into the topic. During our civil
rights lesson where I wasn't acutely aware of the lack of diverse
books in my classroom. Brought into the room we try to merrily
teach the moral of the lesson in that moment and gloss right by.
That as a teacher with a degree in exceptional student education
I have not brought more awareness to my students about those
with exceptional gifts and struggles.

I believe that opening up to our faults and acknowledging
them means we are ready to make the world a more positive

place for our students in the future. This is not a political topic. This is one of bringing awareness to our kids of all the walks of life on this planet, and not just sliding right by due to feeling uncomfortable. If you jumped into this profession then I believe you did it because you want to make a positive impact on the life of a child. To do this we have to shine the light on all the forms of children in the world, and eventually become the light that our kids try to emulate. How do we achieve this?

Tip #9
We Have
To Be The
Game-Changers

When you are able to share your vision and passion with your students then you are achieving the ultimate level of being an influential teacher. You have such a strong ability to make a positive change in the world simply by focusing on the children within the four walls of your classroom. Yes, when you teach with kindness it reflects that value, but there has to be more than just that. There has to be an intentional reason behind everything we do, and every moral of the story we intend to teach.

In one of my earlier years of teaching, my class ended up being partnered with one of the self-contained classrooms. We were there to read along with the students and that opportunity would rotate each week with a different student pair being asked to step up. In the initial meeting one of my mischievous friends, we will say, said a comment that made the tips of my ears turn red. He had whispered to one of his buddies in the class, "that the kid looked really weird," and giggled at them from the back of the group. It was loud enough that we all heard it the teachers, paraprofessionals, the class, and worse of all the students. I'm sure it's safe to say I was mortified.

It would've been so easy to take him out of the rotation with the others who got to have the opportunity to leave class and read, and part of me really wanted to. However, I knew that it would teach him nothing and so I forced him to go. I knew that part of him was also a bit sheepish at being caught with those words said aloud, but away he went. This was a learning opportunity that clearly, he'd not had to maneuver before. At the end of the 30 minutes he and another student merrily skipped back into the classroom. I asked him how it went, and he said he had a great time. Even the teachers from that class said he'd done really well.

Eventually in the weeks that followed the teachers from the self-contained classroom came on a break to our class to talk about the disabilities that the students in their class had. They explained what that meant, how that effected their learning, and why their communication was stilted. My students were so intrigued by adults sharing with them the questions they had been silently pondering themselves. They learned so much about inclusion and those with disabilities that the invisible bridge was built in their minds in how to handle situations they find themselves in the future. That is how we break the mold to creating a world that is better tomorrow than today. We have to be open to the tough communications and questions.

The How-To Embrace The Uncomfortable

9.1 Don't Just Give, Teach

Around Fall each year there is the typical school can food drive. We've all seen it, and maybe even did it in our grade school years. Classes sometimes are even pitted against one another to see who can collect the most cans. I have vivid memories of brown paper bags and boxed food piled high in the corner of my classrooms, but in my head at the time it was connection more so to competitions within the school and the glossed over phrase, "It's for those in need." If you'd asked me at my young age to explain beyond that, I would've been at a loss.

It's a beautiful thing when we show being servants to others in our classroom, but it's even greater when we explain the purpose to our students. If we were to teach them the why beyond the give, then that small action can create a future patron to that charity. We also have to top making these collections of any materials based on competition. I understand the reasoning behind it, because schools want more goods donated. However, why do you want your students to give? If it's because you want them to genuinely care, then winning cannot be involved.

Maybe take a tour if your students are old enough to sort goods at the Manana Food Bank or go and read to the elderly at the retirement home. Have them sit and really see the impact that their time and compassion can do. Explain to them why these places are in place. It's amazing how fired up kids get when it comes to service if you give them the opportunity.

9.2 Diversify Your Library

It's so easy to have a library that holds very little when it comes to diversity in your classroom. We as educators have the responsibility to open our students' eyes to the world, and the easiest way to do that is through books. I have below 25 books that are must-add additions to your classroom library to open new conversations and build bridges with your students.

- ◆ *The Proudest Blue* by Ibtijaj Muhammad
- ◆ *Hidden Figures* by Margot Lee Shetterly
- ◆ *Esperanza Rising* by Pam Muñoz Ryan
- ◆ *White Water* by Michael S. Bandy and Eric Stein
- ◆ *Jabari Jumps* by Gaia Cornwall
- ◆ *Hair Love* by Matthew A. Cherry and Vashti Harrison

◆ *The Day You Begin* by Jacqueline Woodson and Rafael López
◆ *I Can Do Hard Things: Mindful Affirmations for Kids* by Gabi Garcia and Charity Russell
◆ *My Magical Choices* by Becky Cummings and Tamara Rittershaus
◆ *The Sandwich Swap* by Queen Rania of Jordan Al Abdullah and Kelly DiPucchio
◆ *Chocolate Milk, Por Favor: Celebrating Diversity with Empathy* by Maria Dismondy, Nancy Day
◆ *Lailah's Lunchbox: A Ramadan Story* by Reem Faruqi and Lea Lyon
◆ *Malala's Magic Pencil* by Malala Yousafzai and Kerascoët
◆ *Fry Bread: A Native American Family Story* by Kevin Noble Maillard and Juana Martinez-Neal
◆ *One Big Heart: A Celebration of Being More Alike than Different* by Linsey Davis and Lucy Fleming
◆ *Enemy Pie* by Derek Munson and Tara Calahan King
◆ *Maddi's Fridge* by Lois Brandt, Vin Vogel
◆ *Young Water Protectors: A Story About Standing Rock* by Aslan Tudor, Kelly Tudor
◆ *Just Ask!: Be Different, Be Brave, Be You* by Sonia Sotomayor and Rafael López
◆ *Hey A.J., It's Saturday!* by Martellus Bennett
◆ *Sulwe* by Lupita Nyong'o and Vashti Harrison
◆ *Whoever You Are* by Mem Fox and Leslie Staub
◆ *Chocolate Me!* by Taye Diggs and Shane W. Evans
◆ *We Are Family* by Patricia Hegarty's
◆ *Last Stop on Market Street* by Matt de la Peña

9.3 Don't Speak Out of Frustration

This seems like something that is obvious, but I've seen and experienced it enough working with children for over the last decade to know it's not. A child says something that is rude and seems hostile about another child or person. Your face is now flushed, and you cannot believe they'd say such a thing. You react and show frustration at their comment, and now they are upset and the whole teachable moment is gone. It's so easy to let our emotions get the best of us on sensitive topics.

While I could've, and probably did a bit, shown my frustration at my student for his words to him and his reaction I tried not to. He hadn't been taught any better, and thus those words were completely okay to say in his mind. We are fortunate enough to at some point have a loving hand to guide us through new situations with people unlike ourselves. To correct us, educate us, and steer us (hopefully) toward kindness and compassion. When we hold in our frustrations and use them moment to reteach, we are creating more than just a teachable moment. We are helping in creating understanding and a bridge in that child's mind on how they handle those that are not like them and how to address something you may not understand. Then they can go off and be knowledgeable and do their best to show empathy to others.

9.4 Share Your Passions

There is no better way to diversify yourself as an educator than placing in your classroom the passions that inspire you. We all have some form of service or belief that lights us up. Maybe you have a passion for animals, the environment, mental health, homelessness, etc. When the world of your classroom can feel a bit small imagine opening it up to a passion of yours that brightens your day?

For example, if you love animals have your students collect items for dogs, baking dog treats, or going to the shelter to read to animals. The options for your passion to be immersed in your classroom are endless, and sometimes just what you need when you want a break from thinking about subtraction. Here are some other ways you can explore other service ideas in your classroom.

Healthy Eating

◆ Have your students make a salad using fractions or counting for the ingredients.

◆ Grow herbs in clear containers to see the roots for life science.

◆ Students can write recipes for practicing transitional phrases.

◆ Have students add up calories for three- and four-digit addition, and then you can subtract that for daily total for subtraction.

◆ Have your students log their exercise during your human body unit.

Environment

◆ Start an initiative to recycle in your classroom

◆ Grow plants

◆ Learn about water conservation and the water cycle

◆ Have a recycling craft project where students and their families build something using their recycled materials.

◆ Upcycle a bench, old newspaper rack, or wood to create something for your school playground area

Anti-Bullying Campaign

◆ Have students wear a certain color, usually blue, several times a year to promote anti bullying

◆ Have students sign a petition saying they are against bullying

◆ Promote weekly activities that encourage mindfulness, confidence, and empathy for others

◆ Have a kindness week where each day is dedicated to showing gratitude to others (first responders, office staff, organizations in your town, etc.)

9.5 Enrich and Explore

If we want to be the educators that we set out to be when we got our certification, then we need to create an environment that is enriched in other cultures, experiences, and lessons. We have to be open to bringing the outside world into our classroom.

I will never forget in second grade my teacher reading us the book *Too Many Tamales* and then making us tamales to try in the crock pot in our classroom. It was the greatest experience and a food that I never would've thought to try! I remember being excited for weeks at the thought of trying this magical food called "tamales." She brought in a different culture to our classroom and we loved it! It's still something that sticks with me today.

In COVID I took my kids weekly on virtual field trips. We went to Egypt from a video I found online, learned to write in hieroglyphics, and toured 3D tombs of the pharaohs. My students were all about it! We did similar experiences with the Great Wall of China and writing in Chinese symbols, and all day I received pictures of my kids writing symbols all over their papers. A simple 15-minute field trip created a desire to learn more about another culture!

Sometimes these experiences are the only ones of their kind our students experience, and so they are reliant upon us when it comes to learning about the world. If we want to be our best selves as educators and create a platform for success for the next generation, then we have to be willing to put ourselves out there for our students. We have to create a whole world of possibilities within the classroom.

The reason that I felt compelled to write this chapter is because I think as educators we early on sell ourselves short. We believe that our jobs are limited to the standards in our books and the hours we are given, but I want you to remember you are so much more than that! You may be teaching the next game-changer. Maybe a student who impacts the world in a positive way, and it could all start from that small lesson you thought nothing about. We have such an obligation to these kids to realize this, and act on it. So, what kind of teacher are you going to be? One that lets this beautiful opportunity fly by or are you going to change the game?

10

Embrace Our YOUnique Selves

What is it about me that sets me apart?

There is nothing more suffocating as a teacher than conforming to a mold that someone has set for us. We are blessed to be in a job where creativity is the key, and yet sometimes in the wake of curriculum and expectations we lose that. So when we finally let loose and begin to embrace what we bring to the table of education, it can be the most freeing feeling.

I'd mentioned earlier that as I set out on my own grade level in my current job I felt the freedom to run second grade however I so chose. There were so many ways I could run with that opportunity. It's easy as teachers to compare and look at others and wonder if we should be doing the same thing. If they have a certain behavior plan, should we be doing the same? Everyone in my school has their desks in groups, should mine be the same way? You'd think after we got out of college and high school we wouldn't measure ourselves against others so much, but I find sometimes in teaching we do it more than ever. I would beat myself up for not being like someone else.

In my second year, there was a teacher at my school who was so creative that I am still mesmerized years later. She literally created a classroom to look like a base camp at Mount Everest. She even had requested the portable she moved into over her perfectly located room to add to the feel of her theme. There we tiny flags hanging from the ceilings, a pray where that would rotate as it spun outside, and jewels the students could earn for positive behavior. To top it off she had specifically designed polos with her class logo custom designed on them and they rotated in color to match the flags hanging from her ceiling. She wore these rain or shine each week through the year. I stood in wonder at the ability to dive so deeply into creating your own unique style that I couldn't imagine being brave enough to do so.

In fact I would say that my first rooms really didn't have a resemblance of me at all in them. I had the same rules, design, and procedures as everyone else. I didn't sing songs, even though I had a love of music and had done musical theatre for years. Even if it is just walking down the hallway to art. As I packed up my classroom at my first school to move to the beach I didn't feel like anything I was packing felt like me. So I was determined to find my groove at my next school and put myself a bit more into my classroom.

I'd say my first year at my new job I still played it rather safe. My room was a bright-colored pineapple themed and the decor and ideas were rather simple. The only addition being a bench in my curated book nook with hand-sewn seat cushions. I was like a toddler teetering on the edge of a swimming pool, unsure if I should do anything else. I had so many ideas in my head. Of course, I talked myself out of them. I thought, "I don't want to be thought of as that weird and crazy teacher." So safe I played it. The room felt a bit more like me. For dress up days I kept it basic and didn't go all out. I did everything just enough to be fun but still blend in but after that year, I thought, you know what? I want to be different and try something new! I pulled up my big girl pants and embraced my super weird side.

I have a joke with a coworker that when I tell our principal one of my crazy ideas if he looks at me like I have two heads, then I know it's a good idea. First, I brought in a couch, then a coffee table with cushions created a workspace, placed yoga balls around my teacher table, and eventually begged my husband to build me a stage in front of my board. The simple additions of pineapple I had decorated my room with became my thing. I even wore a bright pineapple skirt on the first day. My room radiated my favorite colors and fun side. It felt more like a home away from home. That is when I knew I was on the right track.

Dressing up, weird voices, and oddball thinking became my day today. I created beach themed teams in our class-based off of Ron Clark, and we wore our team shirts on Wednesday's proudly. On Halloween, I spray painted my hair orange and dressed as Miss Frizzle with a chameleon stuffed animal glued to my shoulder. I had officially become that teacher. During Dr. Seuss's week, a coworker said to a student on Wacky Wednesday, "I feel like I'm the only one who dressed up." The student said, "oh, wait till you see Mrs. McKinney." The additions to my room over the years became quirky and different, and even when my student's parents meet me for the first time I tell them, "my class is a bit quirky." I embrace who I am and roll with an odd idea that comes to mind because we should all:

Tip #10
Embrace
Our
YOUnique
Selves

Now, I'm not saying you need to be a wacky teacher that sprays their hair multiple colors a year. That is simply who I am. I am a former theatre gal who loves to have fun. Each of us at my school is very different. Our fourth grade teacher has this wonderful calm vibe and a coffee shop type feel of a room and the kids adore her. She knows who she is, and she doesn't change that for anyone. That is what I mean in this tip.

Look at yourself and what you enjoy. The themes and ideas you have that bring you joy and excitement, and then run with it. Do you love Harry Potter? Then do a measurement lesson and make some smoothie potions. Do you want to dress up like a historical character for a history lesson? Rock that hoop shirt or crazy wig! However, if you aren't like that and you just want to calmly teach and never dawn more than a school shirt then that's great too! We cannot compare ourselves to one another and what we believe the world thinks is the best way to be a teacher. You do not have to be the teachers we see featured on Good Morning America singing and teaching their kids through dances. **You are where you should be as you are.**

This life isn't worth living when we try to fit into the mold others set for us. When you do that you will feel heavy and deflated. When I didn't let myself be the teacher I dreamed of being, because I felt that was too scary and I was worried about judgment then that is where I hated my job. I felt bored and lackluster. I dreaded driving to work each day, but when I tried to figure out a career outside of teaching that I could do nothing seemed to fit. I couldn't understand why I felt so lost. It was because I was too concerned with how the world saw me, and not about how I saw myself. So how do we find that version of ourselves that is true to our unique selves?

The How-To
Be
Yourself &
Love It

10.1 Get Rid of the Judge (Hint: It's You)

I'm sure you've heard it say that we are our own worst critic. I wholly believe that this is true, and that no one is quicker to rip us apart than our own selves. If you don't believe in what you are capable of then why would anyone else? It all goes back to that idea of selling yourself and you are worth it all. So, you need come to terms with that. Find the pieces of you that you love. Maybe it's your humor or the way that you make someone smile with your kind words. Whatever that is take it and run with it.

Similar to finding your best feature in an outfit you have to do the same with your teaching. Are you proud of the way you can truly explain a math concept? Then revel in that ability! If you are a naturally gifted decorator in a classroom like your own educational version of Joanna Gaines then flip that classroom! You have to love the pieces that make you proud and give yourself understanding and grace versus shame on the pieces that aren't your strong suit yet.

You wouldn't judge a baby just making its way in the world, or a student that is just learning to write for the first time, and so why do we talk down to ourselves when we try new things in the classroom? Tell that internal judge to take a hike, and love yourself a lot more.

10.2 Find Your Word

I have a strategy I do every year, and each new season in an organization when I am leading. I sit back and find one work that I want to implement in my life that year. Back in 2017 when I was just getting out there and meeting new people my word was, intentional. Every time I met someone new I intentionally made sure to learn their name, who they were, and to reach out sometime in the future. I wrote notes to people that I random sent in the mail and each new decision was centered on the word. It was a great centering though that helped me make many positive decisions in that year. In 2020 I had chosen the word grace, and I can safely say that after COVID I have certainly had to give myself a lot of that.

We can do the same in the classroom, and you have a page in your book to write this on. What is your word that you want to live and display in your class? First it's all about selecting the word and the reason why. What is it about this adjective that aligns with what you want? Yes, I'm aware that has a completely Zen and doing yoga vibe. However, it does help. Then you go about brainstorming all the ways that this word shows itself in your classroom. Once you have an idea of how you want to resemble this word during your school year just hold onto it.

At the end of the year pull out your brainstorming sheet and see if you learned to be more like that adjective you selected this year. In what ways did you meet your expectations and where did you grow and learn? It's such a great tool in school, life, and in relationships. So find the word that speaks to you.

10.3 Love the Mess

I tell my students and fellow teachers that I am a hot mess express, and I completely am, but there is more to my idea of loving the mess. Let's be completely honest, teaching is one big mess. We deal with the bumps and bruises of children's lives and our own and we trudge through the unknown. Never more true than during remote learning with COVID. We wipe noses, tie shoes, and come home with pen and marker stains on our new shirts. We are literally in the messiest state when it comes to teaching. However, that's what is so wonderful about being who we are.

I worked at Merrill Lynch as a secretary for a financial advisor. I looked around the room during my days loathing the grey walls and stiff pant suits. I craved flair pens and sun dresses. I realized that I didn't want the firm structure of the office world. I was meant to be hap hazard in the educational one.

To me us embracing that messy side of ourselves helps us tap into the part that makes us who we are. We choose to live in the mess and if you are jumping to join in then I can safely say you are meant to be here. Enjoy the badges of honor of the pen marks on your shirt. You are killing it.

10.4 Close the Door

In my mind's eye I can see some of you that are new to the field. Your brain won't shut down from what you saw in school that day. Laminate remnants are littering the floor of you home. Your heart is full with love for your students but also fraying at the painful experiences you may have seen or heard them say. Teaching is a job that never really leaves you.

I know that as you exit the doors of your school, you'll want to ponder those kids of yours and wonder what more you can do. I've sat and prayed with other educators who were literally making themselves sick over it. While I know that it's impossible to close that door sometimes, I believe that to truly embrace you that you have to guard your heart and walk away.

Whatever it is that makes you joyful and happy, you need to find it. Even in the worst of those days. You can't give yourself or those you love 100% when you are carrying burdens with you. As you get in your car either cry it out or listen to music to soothe your soul. Whatever it is that can mend your tired heart. Then remember yourself and your reasons and return tomorrow.

10.5 Embrace Gratitude

I know that being thankful sometimes is tough. Especially on those days after nasty words or tiring comments. However, part of loving who you are is also embracing what you should be grateful for. You sometimes have to reflect on what fills your heart even if it's sometimes hard to remember that.

As you wake up in the morning and before you go to sleep pick a couple of things that you are thankful for. It can be like a salve on the bad days and help you remember the positives when you honestly might not want to. You can also write out a list of all the blessings in your life and look at it once each day, and remember what a lucky person you are.

As you think on these things you can find peace and comfort in knowing who you are, what you stand for, and what kind of teacher you want to be. Then you can branch out and find the teacher in you that you always dreamed of being. You can't be unique when you aren't in tune with yourself, because there will be people and occasions that try to tear you down.

People will judge you whether you want them to or not. One day dressed in my finest deer costume my car broke down and I had to take an uber to school in my costume. I wish I could have shown you this driver's face. There have been parents who don't like my quirky class and wish I was more traditional. I've had a parent tell me she likes another teacher more, and that she has a better style. That's the thing. People aren't always going to like you. That is completely fine. I've heard before that for every five people that you meet, one isn't going to be a fan of you. If you're a people-pleaser like me, that fact can really bug you. Heck, maybe you reading this are the one in five who aren't liking me right now. The thing is though, I have learned (and am still learning) that I can't and don't care. What matters is that my students are happy, loved, and learning. That is our job as teachers, and whatever style you have that is all that really matters at the end of the day.

If you are trying to mold yourself after someone then maybe that's where you find that dread of work or lack of pizazz in your lessons. Are you being your most authentic teaching self? If you aren't then know that there is more, and you have the ability to find it. Go out and look for workshops and see where you gravitate toward. Walk around a teacher shop or website and see what theme catches your eye. Maybe talk to that mentor or friend and ask what they love about you. Maybe that could be the trait or skill you bring into your room. You can pull out the Pinterest boards and tell yourself to pin anything you love and go for it. Remember though, you are more than your classroom, and your mental health is important too. Take breaks where needed, and know that it might take time to find your niche. However, when you take control of who you are as a teacher, then a world of possibilities is there waiting.

11

Never Stop Learning

Where do I go from here?

As I said earlier, putting yourself into a room full of excited educators is the greatest gift you can give yourself as a teacher. The energy is life-giving and can give you a pep in your step as you prepare for your next lesson or school year. I've had a fellow educator once tell me, "once I am no longer eager to learn new skills in my classroom, I know that it's time for me to leave the field." This is an honest and thoughtful answer when it comes to our development as teachers.

I'll come out and say it. You do not know everything. You are not the best in your field, and you have so much more you can learn. This is something I tell myself too. Though by grabbing books as you are now, I know that you know this. You may have even rolled your eyes at my statement. I say this because honestly sometimes there are people who just need to hear it because we all have to consistently change with the ebb and flow of our class. You know exactly who I'm talking about. There's a representative from a new text book company or someone for a training at your school and this person is the first to roll their eyes. They really dislike change and if the book that's literally falling apart has done the trick for decades then why bother!

Even if the routines you've used for a few years work, that doesn't mean you should stick with them. I have painfully seen teachers, or even myself, try to teach in a style or way that doesn't work for the kids they currently have. Behavior plans I have used may work wonders with one group, and do nothing for another. It can be so humbling to a teacher when they feel like they are a first-year teacher again, trying to figure out the ropes like they are new. Honestly I feel like every year I am still starting all over again.

When parents come into my orientation I tell them, even if you've had a sibling in my class you may find this year is different. I change what I do from year to year to meet my students where they are. That's what we have to do as educators. We have to continually change and grow from year to year. Some years I have had more project-based learning and some years my kids have needed a bit more hand holding. You'll have the classes that want all the toughest questions in math and some who cry when you do just basic math facts. So each years class becomes its own story and fits in it owns category all its own.

In theatre, they say that you have to give the illusion of the first time. Meaning that each show should be given the same thought and effort as it was opening night because for that audience it is their first time seeing the show. As educators, we have to do the same. It can be our thirteenth-year teaching, but for that student, it's their first year in that grade. Especially with technology and a new curriculum, we have to do things differently. This year with COVID we all faced challenges in having to rapidly grow and learn. While that was extremely stressful, I do think that it pushed us to think beyond your classroom and in the long haul that can be helpful. I learned new skills that normal I wouldn't have considered, because I "virtually" had no option. This is something that will be consistent, that we always have to remember in our approach to education. Those things will never be predictable, and we have to figure out how to deal with that.

I know we all have that educator in our lives. The one we look back and pray we are nothing like when it comes to our classroom. I imagine the teacher from Charlie Brown, where when they talked it came out in a dull tirade. They may have just had you read a book, or their lessons were maybe a little less than exciting. You'd drag your feet to their class and pick up the pace when it was over. Maybe you didn't have the dull teacher, but you had the one that just never budged. It was their way or the highway. Their books and materials felt dated, and they weren't willing to give an inch when it came to change. I have had a teacher that embodied this, we will call them Mrs. Brown, that pops into my head.

We would come up through elementary school shaking in our kid's with the thought of having her as a teacher. She was tough, she wasn't the most loving, and she wasn't someone you jumped for if you got her as a teacher. I'm not saying that to be cruel, that was just the reality of our situation. Now one thing she was good at was getting us to score high on the state test. She could certainly teach content, and that was never in question. Though that also came through with pounds of homework, and a harsh voice and reprimand for behavior in her class. I remember us all sitting in the recess field dreading the bell to bring us all back in. It wasn't the most thrilling school year for me. Yes, we scored really well on the state exams, but we also were jumping for joy when the last bell of the school year rang. Now, I don't write this to wag my finger at my former teacher, but to show an example of when we don't self-reflect.

I know that parents, the PTA, and others asked for her to ease up on the kids. That we were young, not even ten, and we should actually enjoy our time in school. However, in her eyes, there was that state test, and we did well. So why should she have to change? As an educator myself I now understand. That falls back to that grace that I'd mentioned earlier. What she'd done for years worked, and so why should she do anything differently? I wonder if she'd been willing to accept the guidance of others, or any tips and lessons if her class would've been more engaging and fun.

Even if what we are doing in our room works, it may not be for the best of our students. We have to reflect on our whole teaching style. Are they happy, do they love learning, and are they learning? We have to take a bite out of that humble pie and realize that as teachers we really should always be students ourselves. It keeps us fresh and with the current climate of education that's constantly moving at a speedy pace. There is always something to tweak and perfect, and when you do that you'll find you enjoy your job a lot more. So, remember that as educators we should:

Tip #11
Never
Stop
Learning

This is just something that in my heart I feel I need to share and say. None of us are perfect teachers. We all have our flaws, and no one teacher can be good at all subjects, though we can try to consistently improve in them. So, take a moment and sit back and think about your own flaws. What's the subject that when it's that time of the day to teach it you are a little lackluster?

For me, that's always been math. I would find myself super energetic for my reading block, and then after lunch when math rolled around I was feeling less than pumped. It's not that I can't teach math, it was more that I just don't love it. This has always been my weak spot, and I even required tutoring as a child to get help in the subject. Thus I have to work extra hard to improve. That may mean trying new techniques until one clicks, pouring over blogs and Instagram pages, or reaching out to others to find new ways to improve. It's a never-ending wheel of research and practice, but I embrace it and keep going. Once I find that I've gotten a better handle on making that section of my curriculum engaging I truly enjoy teaching it more, and don't mind when that block of time comes around in the day. It makes the day go by a lot faster, and my students are happier and more engaged.

However, it's not just that one subject that I have to work on. It's my whole class experience that my students have, and so I ask those who know best about how I did in my classroom. I have my students conference with me at the end of each year, and I ask what they loved, disliked, and would change about second grade. Kids are extremely honest, and their ideas are the ways I've been able to change my room and teach for the better over the years. They'll tell me what subject was their least favorite, and then I'll look over my plans for the summer tweaking and making changes. I have tried every year to pick one subject that I want to improve in and it's made a tremendous difference. I went from math to science, then phonics, and now I'm reviewing social studies.

It's a great way to self-reflect, and to constantly learn and become a better educator year to year. Summers are my favorite time to recharge, and find those educators that I admire, and learn from their resources and ideas. When you become more confident and work towards your best self, your pride in your work and love for your job increases tenfold. Me kicking myself in the butt, and working towards becoming a better educator, is truly the tip that has changed my mindset at work. Teachers are like craftsmen. We add tools to our box, we perfect the way we work, and then we get to sit back and admire all that we created in our career.

The How-To
Set Happy Goals
&
Any Skill Can Be a
"Teacher Skill"

If there is something I am all about it's goal setting! I am an enneagram type three which means I am an achiever, and I want to get everything done. Just like when you have the goal to get healthy you break it down and find the tips, tricks, and resources to help you get there. Maybe you sign up for a Weight Watchers class to have some motivation or Crossfit to force yourself to move. So goals in education can be similar. You figure out what you want from that year, and then find a way to make it happen. However, first you need to find the right goal. I know that as teachers we have the diehard goals that all teachers have.

1. That our students feel loved.
2. They learn all they are supposed to.
3. They enjoy their year in your class.
4. They do well on their test
5. Your students become better people while in your class.

Yes, it's amazing for us to have goals when it comes to our kids. However, do you notice anything about those goals? They are the kind that you should have every year and they typically don't change. Which is wonderful, because we do care about our students. However, new yearly goals for us as teachers can help us align where we spend our time. For example, this year I may want my students to learn more about engineering and applying that in science. This calls for me as the teacher to also improve in my knowledge of the skill and how to share it with others. Your yearly goal should influence your students as well as you as the teacher. So how do we feel when we achieve a new goal? We do so happily! Which is exactly what I want you to remember.

Honest
Achievable
Plan
Practice
Yes!

- ◆ Honest- The first thing you need to do to find a good goal for your year in teaching is be honest with yourself. Where is an area that as a teacher you can improve in? Identify that skill whether it be a particular subject area or strategy and write that down.
- ◆ Achievable- Is this something that you can actively achieve this year? How much time is it going to take and can you give that? This is where honesty is still required,

because sometimes being honest with how much time we have to give to achieve the goal is important.

◆ Plan- What's the plan? This is where you can strategize check points to check in to see how you are doing. Write down the steps that are required to help you achieve your goal. When a goal is broken down into steps it's much more manageable.

◆ Practice- This is where practice makes perfect! You are putting your plan into action, and learning through all the bumps along the way. When you are frustrated you remember this P, "practice," which is where we are expected to make mistakes. Then get back up and keep going till you get it done.

◆ Yes!- You did it! You achieved your goal! Now it's time to celebrate and know that YES! You did it!

In our chapter on time management you've now found that you have a bit of wiggle room in your schedule to pick up a hobby or two. As teachers this is also another way for us to continually learn. You may wave it off and say, "well this is a skill just for me for fun!" However, any skill you acquire can be used in the classroom as well!

During my COVID lock up at home I started playing around with graphic design. I used it mostly for a book blog that I picked up while stuck at home, and found I had a lot of fun picking fonts, designs, and colors. I didn't think much of it until we started our preplanning season for school, and then an idea came to me for an afterschool club. The club is titled, "Girls with Grace," and focuses on girls in third through fifth grade and building up their confidence, empathy for others, and eliminating bullying through activities and books.

With the new skills I had practiced in my hobby of digital art I easily created a poster and got to work designing our afterschool curriculum. I had so much fun and a simple trick I'd learned in my free time was able to make an impact on my school life and eventually on the girls who will join up! Other fun little tricks and skills I learned through the years popped into my lessons and in school activities for example I love having herbs in my kitchen, and so with grant money I was able to purchase an inhome garden for my classroom. Now we can watch plants grow and even use them to cook with.

With school I cultivated a strong love for literature and creating questions for books on my own, and with that skill and practice in 2017 I started a local book club called Positively Pensacola. I am able to take what I have learned from curriculum and reading seminars and I create personal questions based off fictional books for women in our local area. So sometimes those teacher skills do come in handy!

12

Yes, It Is That Hard

Does it ever get easier?

Finally, here is something that I'd love to say to you as we near the end of this book. I greatly admire you. There is something about fellow educators that I love, and it makes me so happy I chose this career path. You chose a job that can be so extremely difficult and can wear you down, but it also is one that is a great gift that you can give to others.

When I chose to be a teacher, I got some harsh words that I'll remember from time to time. "You won't get paid anything. That must've been an easy degree. It must be so fun and easy to work with kids all day." In some colleges receiving a degree in educator is equivalent to a Mrs. degree. Even from those in my circle that I love I have heard moments where they boast about another person's job because it seems so much greater than me being "just" a teacher. Education is a field that sometimes unless you are in it, it is really hard to wrap your mind around what we do. I joke with my husband that the reason I force him to go to our school concerts is so he can genuinely see a glimpse of what my job is like.

A couple of years ago I had a student who was the definition of a hard situation. He would refuse to do work, could barely read, would curl up in the corners when mad, throw tantrums, and run off into the distance until you could catch him. It was like anything I had seen in years. A kid not much shorter than I am throwing essentially a temper tantrum.

I was at a training one time the day of an open house and heard how he had tried to make a run for the busy street. I sat in my break that day incredibly frustrated. I thought, "okay so it's not enough that he's reading four grade levels below, but now he's a flight risk." I was so infuriated with my job for a bit. I thought, "our job is to teach, not solve the impossible." I felt like nothing I could do was going to remedy this situation, and it was only September! How was I going to get through the year?

The first thing that I needed to do in this situation was to get over myself. It's not an easy thing to say to yourself but sometimes it's just necessary. I had to just deal with the fact that yes, this was going to be a tough student, but sometimes those are the most rewarding to reach. Slowly but surely, I figured out what made him tick. I observed and wrote down notes like Sherlock Holmes and Google was my Watson. What were the things that set him off? I figured out it happened during certain partner work and writing. He was frustrated with what he couldn't do and hated feeling like he was so behind. So, I was extra careful during those times. I partnered him alongside kids who were easy going, patient, and not pushy. I would make sure to use my softest of voices in those times.

I learned he was a sweet and funny student when he felt confident and loved. So, I tried to create an environment that helped promote those feelings. I didn't budge when he threw fits, and I let him know when I had reached a point of being done. For example, when he stuck a pencil multiple times through my bean bag chairs. As soon as I saw the holes down the hall to the principal we went! I focused on the fact of what I could control in those 180 days he was with me, and to not focus too much on anger and frustration (even if I felt that from time to time), because sometimes that's all we can do!

Then when the spring arrived, he gave a random speech in class. It wasn't provoked and the day wasn't special in anyway. He spoke about how much he loved school and his teachers here. That he had learned so much, and he never wanted to leave. By the end of the year his behavior had dramatically improved.

Though we had a few fits from time to time, his running habits had all but stopped. On top of that he went from reading on a preschool level and barely writing to finally being on grade level and finishing three-paragraph essays I realized that maybe those moments of running down the hall were worth it. That yes, I wanted to pull my hair out sometimes, but that these little moments made all those crazy times add up to more than a typical calm year. My job was hard, but the stories and lessons I had gained from those trying times are so unique to being a teacher and our experience in education.

So, my tip and last reflection to you is this:

Tip #12
Yes,
It Is
That Hard

Sometimes we need to hear a simple validation that yes, teaching is really freaking hard sometimes! We are asked to go above and beyond in these kids' lives. Our jobs do not always clock out right as the bell rings, heck they rarely ever do. However, my friend, it is SO worth it. Don't sit there and ever let those thoughts in your head about you not being good enough or that another job would be better take over. That's just your confidence and negativity eating away at you. Remember the grass isn't always greener on the other side. It's so easy to get that way, and I've been there a few times myself too while mindlessly browsing other professions. Then I pull out the positive notes that I keep. The ones where they say how much they love my class, me, and how much they learned, and I stick with it. I scroll through pictures of our projects, class parties, field trips, and the days where nothing crazy happened at all. Those little memorabilia are critical on the rough days. My favorite thing to look back with is a book that I select each year for the kids to sign. My first was *Oh the Places You'll Go* and then *The Day the Crayons Quit*. I pick books that bring up some memory that is special to that year. It helps fill my heart when it's just a bit bruised.

There will be days where a parent sends you a rude email, or your kids will act like they consumed gallons of sugar and won't listen. The copy machine is broken, and your pens are out of ink. You may be exhausted, and your creative tank is running low. That is where you have to put on your big girl or guy pants and get moving. These can be those moments of self-reflection, or taking time for yourself, or honestly sometimes just a lazy afternoon with a good Netflix binge. Those moments are critical for anyone when the going gets tough.

However, remember that you are the captain of your life. You choose how you want to spend these precious days and what good you want to leave in the world. In 2019 Forbes stated, "that one in three teachers will quit within the first five years of their career." That to me is heartbreaking because in those throngs of teachers deciding to leave, I see myself as well. I was that person that considered packing it up and leaving this educational world behind. I and others whose dreams were littered with crayons, lesson plans, and field trips can sometimes be so easily dashed. I felt defeated, let down, and just done with the whole process. Maybe you are in the same boat. You have a pile of paperwork that never ends, maybe your kids this year were rough, or you may have an administrator that is a hot mess express. I ask you to look back on all of these tips I used for myself and give it one more year.

I'm not saying anything I have said in this book is magic. Heck, I spent these chapters poking at myself and my own flaws. However, if I can get from the days of hair-pulling, barely cohesive lesson plans, and crying in my car to work to where I love my job daily. Then truly anyone can do it.

Being a teacher is hard. However, those kids will look at you and think that you my friend are the greatest person in the room. You will always be their teacher, from whatever grade you find yourself in, and those memories last a lifetime. You have ten months in your year to make an impact that spans beyond the one year. You have the opportunity to spark change, build confidence, and give grace and love. So, though this job is tough, and we are never truly done, how do you see yourself making a lasting impact on the life of a child?

I was always told that teaching was a hard profession, and I thought I knew what that meant. It's another thing entirely though to go in and actually do it. I kept waiting for it to get easier, and honestly, I'm sorry to say, it really doesn't. There will be years that you don't want to go back to the classroom, and summer seems way too quick. However, next year may be the best one yet. To go back in after those tough times is what makes you strong. Those are the times that you will transform more into the educator you want to be. The more you step up and say, "yes, I want to do this and make a difference," the more it will create in you a passion that is unique to our craft. You have to have the courage to know that your job is hard, but that you are going to do it anyway. You have those kids rooting for you, and though we may not know each other, know I am rooting for you too. Remember, through all the muck and tough days you are a teacher. You got this!

Final Thoughts

As you are now done with this book, I hope that you found a story that resonated with you, or a technique that you can add to your toolbox. Teaching is at the end of the day two parts: a gift and a craft. I truly believe that ours is one of the several few professions that is both. We get to perfect over the years a skill that is wonderful and is as unique as the teacher.

You've read my stories in this book that reflect on all the moments in my career where I made my own fumbles. When I set out writing this I felt slight embarrassment at sharing my stories, and as I went on that became less and less. The reason was simply because of you dear reader, because these stories I feel like I am sharing with a friend over coffee in the teacher's lounge. That maybe you feel a bit of understanding with my stories and take them as they are, the simple misgivings of a young teacher who was overwhelmed and at a loss of what to do.

That girl is still here in the moments where I am over my head in figuring out what to do in my class, and especially in moments with COVID trying to figure out this new way of teaching. However, what has changed is my determination to solve my problems and figure them out. I don't give up and have the confidence that I will figure out the problem and soar.

If you are anxious about the classroom or what the future of education beginning to look like I implore you not to fret. While we cannot change the future of our profession, we can stand in strength knowing there will always be a child who needs a teacher, and that's where you come in. Love on them and don't sweat the small stuff and you will be okay. Thank you for your time in reading these experiences of mine and I hope that you feel a bit less alone in the journey. Good luck in your classroom, and may you have less fumbles than I did and an even more exciting outcome!

Worksheets

Classroom Procedures

o Walking into the Classroom
o Packing Up and Unpacking
o Sharpening Pencils
o Getting a Tissue
o Lining Up
o Hallway Behavior
o Going to the Bathroom
o Center Rotations
o Cleaning Up
o Asking for Help Recess
o The Classroom Library (Checking Out and Browsing)
o Using Technology
o Working with Partners/Groups
o Taking Assessments
o Conflict Resolution
o When They Get Hurt or Sick
o Turning in Work

Lesson Plan

Date: _____

Standard: _____

Objective (Your Why): _____

_____

Materials:

* _____
* _____
* _____
* _____

Higher Order Thinking Questions:

* _____
* _____
* _____
* _____

Map It Out:

_____
_____
_____

A Letter From You!

Welcome Parents and Guardians,

As you read this, I know that you are fitfully preparing your child for their first week back to school. Know that I too am preparing for our exciting year ahead, and so I have something I would like for you to do.

When the rush of that first day is over and done with, I want you to sit back and reflect on all you want for your child to accomplish this year. What are your dreams for your child? Do you have any worries or concerns? What goals or skills would you like for them to master? Then write these out along with your child's interests, likes, and dislikes and send it my way!

You and me? We are on a team together this year! You know your child the best, and so I want to have the insight that only their loved ones can have. I will keep this letter through the year to refer back to. It helps me know what our action plan is, but also who your child is.

This letter doesn't have to be long, and it can be handwritten or emailed to me. That is completely up to you! However, it is such a key in setting up your child for their success in my class. I am eagerly awaiting our year to begin, and I am so thankful to have your child in my class.

With Appreciation,

_____

Date to Turn in Your Letter By: _____

You Can Email Me At: _____

Positive Comments for Your Students:

♡ You have such great ideas!

♡ I appreciate how much effort you give.

♡ You amaze me!

♡ Your creativity is remarkable!

♡ You make me incredibly proud.

♡ You are a great classroom role model.

♡ You are brave.

♡ You are always so considerate of other's feelings.

♡ You have the greatest imagination.

♡ You have the best smile!

♡ Your work is always neat and well done!

♡ I love the way you are always willing to give a helping hand.

♡ You are so inclusive of everyone.

♡ You are always so selfless when it comes to others.

♡ You are open-minded when it comes to trying new things.

♡ I love your motivation to do your best work.

♡ You have an excellent gift for facts!

♡ You are a scientist in the making.

♡ I love your growth mindset!

♡ You are a joyful student, and therefore a joy to teach!

♡ You are going to achieve great things!

♡ You are sensitive to those around you and that is a special gift.

♡ I love how you are flexible when it comes to working with others.

♡ You are a gem!

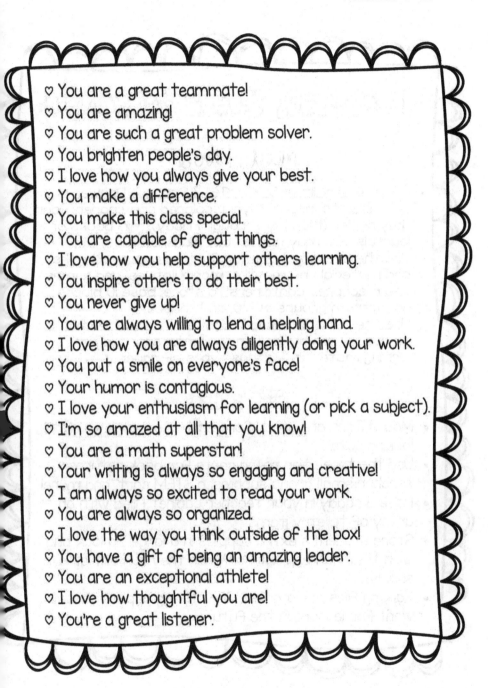

♡ You are a great teammate!
♡ You are amazing!
♡ You are such a great problem solver.
♡ You brighten people's day.
♡ I love how you always give your best.
♡ You make a difference.
♡ You make this class special.
♡ You are capable of great things.
♡ I love how you help support others learning.
♡ You inspire others to do their best.
♡ You never give up!
♡ You are always willing to lend a helping hand.
♡ I love how you are always diligently doing your work.
♡ You put a smile on everyone's face!
♡ Your humor is contagious.
♡ I love your enthusiasm for learning (or pick a subject).
♡ I'm so amazed at all that you know!
♡ You are a math superstar!
♡ Your writing is always so engaging and creative!
♡ I am always so excited to read your work.
♡ You are always so organized.
♡ I love the way you think outside of the box!
♡ You have a gift of being an amazing leader.
♡ You are an exceptional athlete!
♡ I love how thoughtful you are!
♡ You're a great listener.

Teachers Guide to Sanity:

Must Have's!

- Use the Sterilite 13.5" x 11" 9.6" 3 Storage Drawer Organizer to: organize your colored copy paper, your daily copies (Monday through Friday), mini books or journals you may use in your classroom.
- Use the Sterilite 3 Drawer Cart to organize: books and materials by months, manipulatives, and games.
- Use meal prep containers to store: base 10 blocks, counters in groups of 20, and shapes.
- Use the rainbow rolling 10 drawer carts at Michael's to use as: mailboxes for students, storage for writing materials, various types of paper.

Other Tips

- Mason Jars are great for teacher supplies while still looking cute!
- Use the three tier rolling carts for book returns, teacher small group supplies, a STEM cart, and more!
- Have a caddy in your teacher cabinet filled with an array of toiletry items.
- Store student's extra supplies in a large zip lock bag with their names on it for when they run out of a supply.
- Hanging files are amazing for storing papers you will want for lessons in the future.

Embracing Gratitude

Things I'm Grateful For:

- ☐
- ☐
- ☐
- ☐
- ☐
- ☐
- ☐
- ☐
- ☐
- ☐
- ☐

A Moment A Student Brightened My Week:

_____

_____

_____

_____

_____

Ways I Successfully Tackled My Day:

- ☐
- ☐
- ☐
- ☐
- ☐

People That Are a Blessing to Me:

- ☐
- ☐
- ☐
- ☐
- ☐

Something I'm Looking Forward To:

Be
C.O.N.F.I.D.E.N.T

Remember That you Have:

Certifications that you earned.

Opinions that make you unique.

Needs that your students have that you can meet.

Fresh perspective on learning that some may not have.

Ideas that are worth sharing.

Dreams that you have the ability to achieve.

Energy that you can use to positively improve a child's day.

Necessary training to know exactly what to do.

Creativity to come up with new ideas.

Eagerness to help your students do their best.

your Word

Adjective you Want to Embrace

_____

What are 3 reasons you chose this word:

1. _____
2. _____
3. _____

How will you exemplify this word to your students?

_____

_____

How will you persue this character trait?

o _____
o _____
o _____
o _____
o _____

Check In: When do you hope to plan to self-reflect to see how you are doing? _____

I am Worthy

Fill this worksheet in on the days you are feeling you need a pep talk.

1. I know that I am beautiful because:

   _____

   _____

2. I am talented and given the gift of:

   _____

   _____

3. These people are cheering me on in my daily life:

   a. _____

   b. _____

   c. _____

4. I am thankful for so much including:

   _____

   _____

5. Today I am going to inspire a student or friend by:

   _____

   _____

"The only thing between you and big love is your belief in your worthiness of it." – Kristin Lohr

RUBRIC

	Excellent! (4 Points)	Good Job! (3 Points)	We Will Do Better Next Time! (2 points)	I know you can do better. (1 points)

Categories

Total Score: _____/20   Grade: _____ %.

Today's Plan   Date:

To Do List:

- ☐
- ☐
- ☐
- ☐
- ☐
- ☐
- ☐
- ☐
- ☐
- ☐

Notes:

_____
_____
_____
_____
_____
_____
_____

Parents to Contact:

- ☐
- ☐
- ☐
- ☐
- ☐

Copies & Grading:

- ☐
- ☐
- ☐
- ☐
- ☐

After School Necessities:

- ☐
- ☐
- ☐
- ☐
- ☐

Name: _____ Week of: _____
Anything circled is where your child excelled this week!

1. I am a role model:
    A. Acts as a leader in the classroom.
    B. Respects other ideas.
    C. Acts as a role model in the hallway

2. I am responsible:
    A. Comes to the carpet ready to learn.
    B. Follows transitions quickly and quietly.
    C. Waits patiently for others.
    D. Keeps desk area organized and neat.
    E. Completes work without guidance and supervision.
    F. Follows written/oral directions consistently

3. I am cooperative:
    A. Helpful during group activities.
    B. Kind to others.
    C. Includes everyone.

4. I am respectful:
    A. Says please/thank you/you're welcome.
    B. Offers to help adults or peers.

5. I am an achiever:
    A. Takes their time to complete assignments.
    B. Shows their work and thinking on assignments.
    C. Gives extra effort into work.
    D. Takes free time to read

7. I am a participant:
    A. Attentive and ready to learn.
    B. Answers questions in class.
    C. Offers to share ideas and thoughts in class.

9. I am awesome:
    A. Art   D. PE
    B. Music   E. Computer Lab
    C. Library

Points Earned This Week	Citizenship Total
_____	_____/ 100

Date: _____

Circle the rule that you broke:

<u>Be Kind to Others</u>   <u>Eyes and Ears Are Listening</u>   <u>Alert and Ready to Learn</u>

<u>Classmates are Family</u>   <u>Hands & Feet to Yourself</u>

What did you do that doesn't follow school rules?

_____

_____

What would be a better choice?

_____

_____

Parent Signature: _____ Student Signature: _____

Date: _____

Circle the rule that you broke:

<u>Be Kind to Others</u>   <u>Eyes and Ears Are Listening</u>   <u>Alert and Ready to Learn</u>

<u>Classmates are Family</u>   <u>Hands & Feet to Yourself</u>

What did you do that doesn't follow school rules?

_____

_____

What would be a better choice?

_____

_____

Parent Signature: _____ Student Signature: _____

Printed in the United States
by Baker & Taylor Publisher Services

Printed in the United States
by Baker & Taylor Publisher Services